Sort Your
Life Out
Life DIY

Pete Cohen and Sarah Tay

Balloon View Ltd
Brenzett Place
Brenzett, Kent
TN29 0ET
www.balloonview.com

First published in 2011.

ISBN 978-1-907789-12-2

Printed in the United Kingdom for Balloon View Ltd by
CPI Group (UK) Ltd., Croydon, CR0 4YY

A CIP Catalogue record for this book is available from the British Library.

www.balloonview.com

Table of Contents

What is Life DIY?

Welcome to Life DIY. By picking up this workbook you have already taken the first step to transforming your life!

You're probably aware of the current DIY craze to make your home a better place; somewhere attractive and cosy. Life DIY is about doing exactly the same thing, but doing it to yourself. It's a personal makeover that helps you to become more at home with yourself and happier with your life.

This workbook takes you through the Life DIY process, helping you fix, mend and clear out everything that is holding you back. As a Life DIY expert, I am going to help you to undertake a complete overhaul. Together we will dismantle any bad habits and negative emotions. You will be in charge of your feelings rather than them being in charge of you. You will be able to throw out any obstacles that are in your way. Fear, anxiety, lack of confidence, anger, guilt, worry, stress or relationship problems will be a thing of the past. Your life will be bright and sparkling!

For over 20 years I have been using the Life DIY process to help people to meet their potential and realize their dreams. More importantly, I have overhauled my own life so I know what it entails and I know first hand that it works!

DO IT YOURSELF

In 2002 the UK's DIY market was worth more than £23 billion and growing. The National Federation of Builders claims that at the beginning of 2003, one in three homeowners was planning a building project, with the main aim being to increase the value of their property. TV home improvement programmes have made DIY look simpler and sexier than ever before and have made the dream home a real possibility.

Along with refurbishing your home space, there is also an increasing focus on decluttering your belongings and your wardrobe. Makeovers are very 'in'. Our homes and clothes are often an outward expression of our inner world and if you watch any makeover programme, you will see how someone can experience significant inner changes by renovating their living space or revamping their image. They often feel lighter, more in control and have clearer thoughts and an improved image of themselves. And that's just from changing the outside. Imagine what can be achieved when you revamp what goes on inside you!

Would you live in a home that had a beautiful exterior but inside was full of leaks, damp and clutter, with poor wiring and no insulation? We often spend time prettying up our exteriors with the latest trends, make up and style accessories, but inside we live with negative emotions and a poor self-image. This workbook will show you how to tackle these problems and renovate your life.

Many of the people who come to me for Life DIY coaching feel that they've neglected themselves and fallen into disrepair, but it's highly unlikely that they're totally broken. They are functioning and they think that if they carry on as they are, life will just go on in the same way. What they seem to be unaware of is that life can get better and they can be happier. When you Life DIY you begin to see the benefits that can be gained just by making some simple changes. You'll then experience first hand just how much better your life can be.

I've written a wish list of what you can achieve when you Life DIY. Tick the ones you want:

☐ To be happier

☐ To have more confidence

☐ To feel more positive about life

☐ To break unwanted habits

☐ To have better relationships

☐ To feel healthier

☐ To realize my full potential

☐ To feel better about myself

☐ All of the above

WANTS AND NEEDS

What may become apparent, as you continue to read, is that what you want isn't necessarily what you need. Have you ever been shopping and stopped yourself from buying something which you just didn't need? There's a time and a place for unnecessary indulgence, but it's necessary to fulfil needs first.

Sometimes we paint over the cracks of our lives and hope that the shiny new gloss will make us forget what's underneath. You can paint over something a number of times - even so many times as to forget what the original looked like - but as anyone who's done this knows, too many layers of paint will eventually fall off and reveal the true picture - cracks and all. This 'paint over it' school of DIY may seem like the best option at the time: it's quick, easy and feels a bit naughty! But it won't work forever. It's like hiding something under the carpet- eventually it will trip you up. And I guarantee that you don't need any more obstacles in your life.

I want you to come to terms with what you need rather than what you want. And something we all need is to feel at home in our own mind and body. Life DIY can show you how - and more than that, it can bring you a lot of fun in the process and some exciting results at the end!

WHAT'S TO COME?

Let me tell you what's coming next. It's all laid out in 12 steps and it's simple and straightforward. It's like assembling a piece of furniture - everything's there for you, you just have to follow the instructions. So here's a sneak preview of what's in each step:

Step 1 - Getting your toolbox ready ensures you have the right tools to remain positive and motivated.

Step 2 - Interior design helps you create your own master plan, your vision of your bright new home.

Step 3 - Make your house a happy home gives you a starting-point against which to measure your progress towards happiness.

Step 4 - Building on solid foundations delves into the fundamentals that you were born with - the foundations of your life.

Step 5 - Contents valuation helps you look at your own values and expectations and to become a better version of yourself.

Step 6 - Rewiring shows you how to change the way you think in order to be more powerful and positive.

Step 7 - Decluttering teaches you how to clear the clutter and be in charge of your mind rather than it being in charge of you.

Step 8 - Fixing your energy leaks shows you how to keep yourself energised and positive.

Step 9 - The emotional extractor fan teaches you how to let go of things that are stopping you from enjoying more happiness and success.

Step 10 - Tightening your security system banishes insecurities and self-doubt.

Step 11 - How does your garden grow? weeds out negative beliefs and nurtures ones that will support you in your life.

Step 12 - Mental Feng Shui teaches you how to enjoy every single moment of your life.

In order to do a job properly, you need to be well prepared, so first there is a preparation chapter which takes a quick look at what's happened to you to warrant the need for Life DIY. Then you can begin the 12-step programme.

But before we go any further, let's take a closer look at the way the process is designed.

HOW TO LIFE DIY

Changing a light bulb is one of the easiest and quickest jobs you can do, but many people leave themselves in darkness for weeks because they perceive the job to be more cumbersome than it is. If they focused on how quick and simple it was, they'd probably just get on and do it.

The ideas in this workbook are very simple and very manageable. You could sit and contemplate first, but if you really want to see some changes, take the plunge, follow the process step by step and it will be easier than you imagine!

In my experience, we make the best job of things when we are feeling happy. So this workbook is designed to keep you in a positive state for changing, which will ensure that you do the best job that you can of DIYing your life. To achieve this you will need to make yourself more of a priority and to give the process your full attention. You are making a conscious choice to Life DIY and, as with most things in life, the more you put into it, the more you will get out of it.

Apparently 90 per cent of people who read a book don't get past the first chapter. How many people do you know who start projects, never to see them through to completion?

Challenge

My first personal challenge to you is to take the time to read this whole workbook, step by step, and complete each exercise at least once. See yourself as a piece of art that needs restoring.

Although there are 12 steps to follow, you may want to read all the way through the workbook first before you go back and do the exercises properly, or you may choose to dive straight in with the exercises first time through. There is no right or wrong way and only you will know what fits best with your lifestyle and personal preference. There are no time limits and you can always re-read a section or refer back to a point at any time.

I want you to savour this interactive experience. Here are some tips on how to get the most out of it.

TIPS AND REQUIREMENTS

- Have a Life DIY notebook for your thoughts and observations. I want you to use this workbook as much as possible and make it special to you

- Have some post-it notes and coloured pens to hand to personalize your workbook and to highlight key ideas

- When you undertake the exercises, find somewhere free of distraction

- Where possible, follow the steps in order, but if you don't feel ready to do a particular exercise, skip it and come back to it when it feels right for you to do so

- Remember that some exercises will suit some people better than others: if you've tried something a couple of times and it doesn't feel right to you, move on - there's plenty more to do!

- Be aware of your own excuses (e.g. 'I've tried this stuff before', 'I haven't got time', 'There's too much to do', 'I don't see how this can work'). There may be some truth in these, but if you let everything stand in your way, you won't make any changes at all

- Give yourself credit for each step you take, however small. Make sure you write down these personal triumphs in your workbook or notebook

Throughout the workbook you will see a number of headings:

Quick Fix: Something you can do immediately - any time, anywhere

Affirmation: Affirmations are positive statements about you that can empower you, make you feel good and make a significant difference to your change process. I encourage you to repeat these over and over again with conviction

Challenge: These are bigger tasks that you will need to set aside some time for. But they are just as simple and straightforward as the other exercises

Client case study: These are real examples of people I have worked with. You can learn a lot from them

Snapshot: These are based on real experiences, but names or circumstances have been altered for confidentiality. You may find yourself relating to these stories, as they emphasize key points

Convincer: These are snippets of information that will reinforce the conviction that your choice to change is the right one

One To Watch: Throughout the book I will encourage you to watch a number of different films, some of which you may have already seen. It won't do you any harm to watch them again, as all of these films help to promote some key Life DIY messages. I also want you to sit back and enjoy the process of change

Quotes: If any of the quotes in this book inspire you, write them down and put them in a place where you can see them – stick them on a mirror or your fridge or a cupboard door

At the back of this workbook you will see that I have also included my personal story. You can choose to read this at any stage. I hope it will inspire you and help you to see that we can all change, no matter what!

HAVE FAITH

I want you to know up front that some of the things I will be suggesting may feel strange at first or you may not see the point of doing them. All the explanations are in this workbook, but there are some things that won't be explained until after you've done them.

Client Case Study

I have been running weight loss programmes for many years. On one of my courses there was a man who lost nearly two stones over eight weeks. On the last evening of the course he said to me 'It's great! But does the theory add up?' I remember saying 'Pardon?' in shock. This man was living proof that the programme worked, yet he had to know that the theory added up to be totally satisfied.

Whilst there is a theory to back up my weight-loss programme, I told the man that it was backed up by the fact that people

---

succeeded in losing weight and that I
continually refined the process. I told him to
look in the mirror and see that he was living
proof that the theory did add up.

I believe that some things are best tried without
any prior knowledge, so that you really experience
them rather than rationalize or intellectualize
them. I'm asking you, therefore, to trust the
process and to trust me. I will be guiding and
coaching you all the way, so stay with me.

When people DIY their homes, they often need to
leave what they're doing to take a tea break or
rest overnight and come back to it refreshed. Bear
in mind that the same applies to Life DIY, so take
breaks when you feel you need them.

Have faith in the process and more importantly
have faith in yourself. You can do it!

How Did I Get in This State?

What state are you in? The same DIY issues crop up time and time again: damp, insulation problems, loose fittings, dodgy wiring and out-of-date decor. In Life DIY the same problems seem to crop up over and over again too. They're not as obvious as scratched walls or wonky shelves, but as you go through the 12 steps, you will become aware of what's holding you back. The most common Life DIY problems are:

- Anger
- Anxiety
- Blame
- Fear
- Guilt
- Hatred
- Insecurity
- Jealousy
- Lack of self-control
- Low self-esteem
- Obsessive behaviour
- Pessimism
- Sadness
- Stress
- Worry

Most of these happen to us all at some stage and quite often we're totally unaware of where we picked them up. Even though we don't want them in our lives, many of us get comfortable with them, so I call them 'mental comfort zones'. So let's take a look at how we fell into these zones. Then we can see how we can get out of them.

If you were going on a long trip, chances are you'd plan where you were going and how you would get to your final destination. When you set off on your journey through life you didn't have much say initially in which way you were heading. When you were very young a lot of decisions were made for you; what you ate, where you went, which school you attended, whom you spent time with and what you wore. As you grew older, outside influences remained high and the decisions became more important: what you studied, what career you chose, what kind of partner you looked for and what morals and values you lived by. Many of us weren't asked what we wanted. Even though others thought they were acting in our best interests, our choices were often taken away and decisions thrust upon us. It's no wonder many of us ended up heading in the wrong direction.

MODELLING: FOLLOW THE INSTRUCTIONS...

Picture the scene: screws, nuts, bolts, nails and pieces of wood strewn about the floor. And no instructions. Maybe you'd have a decent idea of where to start by following the picture in your mind, but chances are you'd be pretty clueless. There would be a few rogue nuts that just didn't seem to fit and extra pieces of wood left over. In situations like these we rely on instructions for guidance. Even with instructions, you might still be a little baffled as to how to fit things together. But what if you had someone to copy?

Do you remember the family game show The Generation Game? One of the games which entertained the audience the most was when the contestants had to copy an expert. Of course few formal instructions were given to guarantee the most entertainment for the audience. Sometimes life is a little bit like this!

> **The best and fastest way to learn a sport is to watch and imitate a champion.**
>
> Jean-Claude Killy

When we are growing up we are often thrown into situations with little or no instruction and we don't realize that we have choices, so we mimic those around us, usually our families. Just like The Generation Game contestants, we follow their every move.

At such a young age, we haven't begun to filter the information that we receive; we don't analyse or question others. So what if we see Daddy shouting at Mummy, Mummy eating different food from everyone else, big sister rolling her eyes behind Granny's back, Mummy cursing bad drivers, Daddy working long hours and big brother arguing with everyone? As young children we don't know about right and wrong, good or bad, or inappropriate versus appropriate behaviour. We accept what we see as normal and think that that's the way we're supposed to act. And so we learn when to feel angry, sad, worried, jealous or afraid.

COPY CATS

Snapshot

In an art class, 30 children are asked to draw a bowl of fruit. They are all looking at it from different angles, and with their varying degrees of talent and individual styles they produce 30 different works of art. But aren't they all looking at the same thing?

How can two people watch the same film and have totally different experiences of it? How can two people be sitting in the same traffic jam yet one be calm and the other uptight? Our individual experience is subjective and not necessarily like the objective reality that's out there. Everything external to us, whether it's a bowl of fruit, a film or a traffic jam, remains the same and it's our interpretations that differ. We see things differently according to the filters we have in our minds - our values, beliefs, prior experiences and morals.

When we were young children, though, we didn't understand that each person had their own interpretations of life, so we took on the values, opinions and beliefs of those we trusted and admired – our parents, siblings, teachers, best friends and favourite TV personalities, pop stars and sports idols.

A friend of mine became vegetarian at the age of 11 because her sister was vegetarian. She freely admits now that she didn't consider the consequences of what she was doing but looked up to her sister so much that she assumed it must be a cool thing to do!

Many a parent has mused, 'I don't know where you've got that from' in reaction to a surprising outburst from their child, but if they looked hard enough they would find the root of the behaviour. It might even have come from them!

Copying is actually a very effective and efficient way of learning. After all, if you do exactly as someone else does, you've got a pretty high chance of getting it right - assuming they're doing it 'right'! But aren't there some things you have copied that don't do you any favours? Are there any opinions, values, beliefs and negative habits that you think you'd be better off without? It's likely that what you were told as a child has shaped your life, but many of the messages you received may no longer be useful to you and maybe weren't even useful at the time.

Let me give you a common example. Do you always eat what's on your plate? Many of us do because we were told as children that there were starving people in the world and we should be grateful for what we had. So many people learn to clear their plates and override the body's natural instinct to stop when they've had enough. The message was useful once, because it came about during wartime; food was rationed and next week's food was not guaranteed. However, now most of the Western world has more than enough to eat and can access food at any time. The message is defunct, yet, for many, the habit remains. It has played a large role in the obesity epidemic of the West.

Imagine taking a page from an interior decorating magazine or a room from a show house and replicating it down to the tiniest detail. And then, after living in it for a while, you find it seems a bit impersonal, foreign and lacking in homely qualities. Wouldn't it be better to take a general idea and put your own character on it with personal trinkets and original touches? Wouldn't you be more likely to end up with something that you would feel comfortable in? How comfortable do you feel living someone else's life? Do you want to be a clone of someone else, down to their every opinion? Or would you like to be a better version of yourself?

EDUCATION: BUILDING THE FOUNDATIONS

Education forms the foundations of our lives. The dictionary defines it as the system of teaching people, usually at a school or college, or the gradual process by which a person gains knowledge and understanding through learning.

In the children's classic tale 'Alice in Wonderland', Alice has a rather confusing conversation about education with the Mock Turtle and the Gryphon, who both went to a school where the lessons got shorter each day. They explain this to Alice as best they can by saying, 'That's the reason they're called lessons... because they lessen from day to day.'

> **The road to success is always under construction.**
>
> Lily Tomlin

Lessons never end, of course. We're being educated throughout our whole lives. In addition, almost all of us, certainly in the developed world, go through some formal education. On our first day at school we turned up with a backpack with perhaps a packed lunch and maybe our teddy bear. We felt so important because we had a reason to carry a bag like a proper grown-up. We had a bag and we were going to fill it. We put in some knowledge (useful or not), some rules, a hefty pile of self-consciousness, a heavy textbook on not being good enough and a few judgements. Then we sneaked in some expectations to add to the load. By the time we finished our education the backpack had got quite cumbersome but we were so used to carrying it we didn't notice.

What did you leave school with? You may have or may not have left with qualifications, but many of us left without many of the qualities needed to face the real world, qualities that would equip us to deal with failure, guilt, stress, anxieties and other mental comfort zones. Sadly, many of us are only taught what to think rather than how to think for ourselves.

This view can be seen as a bit harsh, as we do learn a lot of useful things at school. We learn about relationships from playground antics and a lot of people form some of their best friendships there. Many of us do, however, also pick up a lot of things that limit our learning and development. Take two different accounts of conventional schooling.

MY STORY

I went to an independent boys' school in north London. I had a short attention span and found it hard to learn through conventional methods. I wanted to run around the whole time and got quite a shock when I had to sit still, listen and not speak unless spoken to. By the age of five I had realised that I didn't fit in with my classmates. Sensing this difference, I sought attention by mucking about and having as much fun as I could. I was assessed as having severe learning difficulties. But whilst times-tables and tying my shoelaces were a struggle, finding something to laugh at was always easy. This sense of being different, of not being capable of learning, instilled severe self-doubt and despite succeeding in sport, I sought out evidence to confirm the belief that I was different. This feeling of alienation was reinforced when I couldn't get into the private school that all my friends were attending and even though I fell into the 'in' crowd at my new state school, I was always the one they teased and bullied - in a friendly way, of course.

I left school with no qualifications but a lot of beliefs. I believed I was stupid and I believed there was something wrong with me. I wasn't allowed to retake my '0' levels because I wasn't considered good enough, or intelligent enough, and I 'couldn't learn'. I was put on a course with all the other supposed no-hopers, but something in me snapped. I knew that inside me I had ability and intelligence like everyone else. I decided to apply myself and started to see results. Five years later I had a degree and a certificate of education (ironic, eh?). And at the age of 23 I finally learned to spell, when I was taught in a way that was appropriate for me.

SARAH'S STORY

Sarah has helped me to write this book and her experience of formal education was very different from mine. When she started at a state primary school, she had just moved to the UK from overseas and felt a little bit different; she sounded different and looked different. To keep from drawing attention to these differences, she spoke only when spoken to, sat still and listened. She happened to be a bright girl and moved on at 11 to a girls' boarding-school, where she continued to excel in all academic areas.

Others' reactions to her results however, made her feel very self-conscious. So she learned to draw attention to her weaknesses and to put herself down. She managed to create her own low self-esteem that acted as a protection mechanism to stop her feeling different. And then she managed to find something that she could really justify putting herself down about: her body. Being one of the earliest developers in her class, she had hips and breasts way before her friends did and felt different from the other girls with their boyish figures. So normal growth and physical change were translated into 'being fat and unattractive' and Sarah took on board the belief that she wasn't thin enough, pretty enough and therefore good enough. This spiralled into eating disorders. Sadly, these beliefs are all too common nowadays amongst youngsters, both girls and boys.

Two very different academic experiences and environments that produced the same belief: 'I'm not good enough.' This common belief doesn't necessarily stem from experiences at school, but chances are the education system doesn't help it. What both Sarah and I were really saying was: 'I want to fit in, I want to conform. It's not nice being on the outside and looking in!' It's ironic that this quest to be like everyone else leads us to be more alien to ourselves.

WHAT'S WRONG WITH US?

Maybe the reason many of us leave school with a sense of underachievement or low self-worth is because it is during this time in our life that differences are most apparent. We attend classes with people our own age and for a lot of the time we have to study the same things and play the same sports as everyone else, so comparisons are really easy to make. Maybe the curriculum doesn't offer the subject or activity in which we would excel. We may be trying our best, but still not make the football or netball team or win the awards at prize days, and so we are left with the realization that we are not the best. In these circumstances, it's easy for our self esteem to fall.

If we carry an unhealthy level of confidence on into the rest of our lives, we will find ways to cement our low self-esteem wherever we go.

Snapshot

Joe jumped out of bed at the sound of his alarm and stumbled into the cold damp bathroom. 'Isn't it funny how your nose always looks bigger first thing in the morning?' he thought as he guided his razor around the contours of his gradually ageing face. 'I wonder how much a nose job costs.

Of course, if I'd got that promotion I went for, I'd have the money to afford a nose job and if I had a smaller nose, I might have got lucky with that girl on Saturday night. Of course, having a fast car would probably have helped and maybe some wittier chat... And I'm sure she said something about hating the way men let themselves go once they get past 30,' he mused as he noticed his gut resting on the edge of the sink.

Joe thinks that if he had a smaller nose, washboard stomach, more cash and some comedy lines that his life would significantly improve. Some of you probably think he's right.

We are fed a lot of information about what's wrong rarther than what's right and so we become very good at following this pattern. We are surrounded by images of supposed perfection and many of us feel we have to meet these standards. We don't often see situations for what they are and we don't often see ourselves for what we are either. Like Joe, we may be taking our feelings of insecurity and using them to colour our whole existence.

FITTING IN

Snapshot

Molly is one year old. She is starting to experience the freedom that comes from walking but she still can't express herself verbally. She wants to be heard, so screams and cries when she feels she's being misunderstood. She doesn't care where she is, what time of day it is, who's there or what they think. She only cares about fulfilling her needs. Why don't these big people get it?

Her sister Katie is nearly three. She is chattering away now and can say most of what she needs to at this age. She doesn't have an expansive vocabulary or an elegant turn of phrase, but it doesn't limit her from speaking up.

Their big brother Tom is five. Today is his birthday. His parents have thrown a party for him and all his classmates have been invited. The room is full of spidermen, firemen, supermen, power rangers, fairies, princesses, nurses and Cinderellas. An entertainer is showing them a plethora of magic tricks and jokes and engaging them with questions. Some of the children call out their answers loud and clear with little thought of whether they're right or wrong; others look shy and coy. It's apparent that these children have already started to learn that getting it wrong is embarrassing and that no self-respecting superhero would risk looking foolish or different.

If we make the assumption that Molly's, Katie's and Tom's experiences are close to the norm, what do we get if we look at teenagers or adults? We see people who are overly conscious of everything they do or say because they feel there's a penalty for being different. We see how, for most people, self-consciousness increases with age. The thought of standing out from the crowd is most people's idea of hell on Earth.

LEARNING TO BE YOURSELF

During a training course I was holding a few years ago, I asked the trainees to come up with an entertaining story to tell the rest of the group. One of them stood up and held up a £50 note for us all to see. She asked us who'd like it and, not surprisingly, we all admitted we would. She then screwed it up in a ball and asked us whether we would still like it? Yes again. She then dropped it on the floor and trampled all over it. On picking it up, she asked us again if we still wanted it? Nods all round. 'So you see,' she said, 'you might be screwed up and you may have been trampled on, but you've still got the same worth.'

What you will be finding out as you go through this workbook is that although your education, your family, culture, religion and other life experiences may have taken you away from the true essence of who you are, you can still realize your true potential. You may think of yourself as a crumbling ruin, but with a little restoration, you'll be fine. But first, let's see what you need to get rid of.

Challenge

WHAT'S WEIGHING YOU DOWN?

One exercise I do with all my clients is to get
them to imagine that they have been carrying
their school backpack all their lives and that
they've added to it along the way. The thing
about backpacks is that when they're firmly
attached to our backs they are always behind
us, follow us around, and can be hard to
put down. It's also difficult to reach behind
ourselves to delve inside and offload things - as
much as you try to grab what's in there, you
just go round in circles like a dog chasing its tail.
I have listed below some of the most common
burdens that you may be heaving around in
your backpack. I want you to mark down to
what extent you experience them. Just go with
your intuition on this. I don't want to know what
you're feeling right now but what you think you
carry with you a lot of the time.

Not at all	A Great Deal
Anger	0 1 2 3 4 5 6 7 8 9 10
Anxiety	0 1 2 3 4 5 6 7 8 9 10
Blame	0 1 2 3 4 5 6 7 8 9 10
Fear	0 1 2 3 4 5 6 7 8 9 10
Guilt	0 1 2 3 4 5 6 7 8 9 10
Hatred	0 1 2 3 4 5 6 7 8 9 10

Not at all	A Great Deal
Insecurity	0 1 2 3 4 5 6 7 8 9 10
Jealousy	0 1 2 3 4 5 6 7 8 9 10
Lack of self-control	0 1 2 3 4 5 6 7 8 9 10
Low self-esteem	0 1 2 3 4 5 6 7 8 9 10
Obsessive behaviour	0 1 2 3 4 5 6 7 8 9 10
Pessimism	0 1 2 3 4 5 6 7 8 9 10
Sadness	0 1 2 3 4 5 6 7 8 9 10
Stress	0 1 2 3 4 5 6 7 8 9 10
Worry	0 1 2 3 4 5 6 7 8 9 10

What I'm going to tell you now is very important:

1. You were not born with these ways of behaving.

2. You learned how to do them.

3. Chances are, you're pretty good at doing them

4. To get rid of them, you must replace them with something else.

So how prepared are you to do something about them? What does your gut instinct say?

> *The winners in life think constantly in terms of I can, I will and I am. Losers, on the other hand, concentrate their waking thoughts on what they should have or would have done or what they can't do.*
>
> Dennis Waitley

Clients will often say to me 'I bet you've never met anyone like me before' or 'I suppose I'm the most messed up person you've ever seen? ' Well, sorry to break the news to you but each and everyone of us experiences difficulties and we all suffer emotions that we don't want. We're all alike in this. What makes someone stand out is his or her determination to change.

I want you to go against the grain and stand up for what you want. The classic British reserve means that we are often held back from believing in ourselves. It's simply not the done thing to rate yourself as someone amazing, without the risk of being put down as a bighead or as being vain. Learning who you are and believing that you can be even greater, is a vital defence to many of the stresses of modern life. Just because other people are happy to keep themselves weighed down, doesn't mean you have to as well. I want you to be positive about offloading these mental weights and I want you to know that you can change.

> **Everybody is born with an equal chance to become just as unequal as he or she possibly can.**
>
> Anonymous

What I am encouraging you to do in this workbook is to examine the journey you've taken so far in your life, what you've collected that you don't need any more and the direction you'd like your life to go in now. You aren't necessarily bound to all the options you've taken in the past: when you take a wrong turning on the road, there is always a way back or the chance to take a different route, even if it means going around the roundabout a few times or getting lost in a oneway system first.

One more thing I want you to realize is, that you always have a roof over your head; throughout this process you are totally safe.

Affirmation
I'm safe: it's only change.

Write down this affirmation on one of your post-it notes and place it somewhere to remind you to say it over the next few days. Say it with conviction, as if you really mean it!

You should mean it - it's true. And this process will make you feel even safer inside yourself and you will discover the warm, insulated feeling that comes from feeling happy and secure with yourself.

You've come a long way in life and survived. You may have gone to many different places and done many different things. Whatever you have done, your experiences have probably left you with a legacy of beliefs, expectations and habits which all affect the way you are now. You've collected some unnecessary clutter and bits of you have fallen into disrepair. Isn't it time to get rid of all this and restore yourself to your full glory?

Let's start your DIY programme by making sure you've got all the tools you'll need.

Chapter I
Getting Your Toolbox Ready

Through my experience of working with people, I have learned that any life change requires commitment and enthusiasm to be successful. Some people are wary about making changes because of what they might find out about themselves or because it might be hard work, and these concerns are only to be expected. One of the first things I do to put my clients at ease is to help them appreciate that it's OK to have imperfections and insecurities - as you now know, we all pick them up just through growing up. But we can all change. It's true that any process of change contains an element of the unknown, but the unknown can be exciting and liberating too.

As I said earlier on, many people buy books with good intentions only to cast them aside, usually because they are asked to do something that requires more effort than they are prepared to give. Before you go any further, I want you to read and digest this section and consider whether you are prepared to do what's suggested.

A GOOD WORKMAN USES THE RIGHT TOOLS

To make changes effectively you need the right tools. In fact you need an entire toolbox filled with tips, challenges and strategies. You already have most of the tools you need to make your life happier and more fulfilling, but they may be buried underneath outmoded habits that you have collected along the way and they may be a little rusty from lack of use. All you need to do is dig them out and sharpen them up and then you'll be ready to start. Let's look at what you need.

MAKE A COMMITMENT

Remember that the people who make significant changes are those who are prepared to do things differently, to make themselves a priority and not to take themselves too seriously! So make a conscious choice to change your life for the better and as you read through this chapter, tick the boxes by the statements to make a commitment to yourself. Alternatively, you could copy the statements into your Life DIY notebook as a regular reminder of your commitment. As I will be asking you to note down several things as you go through the book, it would make it easier to have your special notebook to hand. Honesty is always the best policy, so, as your first tool ...

☐ **I'm honest with myself**

THE POWER TOOL

In DIY the power tool is the most effective tool. It's the centrepiece of any tool box - it allows you to finish a job quickly and efficiently and is very versatile. Some people are afraid to use something so powerful, but you just have to learn how to do it. It's like learning to drive: it's strange at first but there seems to be a defining moment when you realize that you are controlling the car rather than the car controlling you. You can use the brakes or the accelerator as you please and steer in whatever direction you want to go.

With Life DIY it may seem strange at first to leave behind your mental comfort zones. Any change will be unfamiliar and the process can seem daunting. Often this is just the result of your own expectations. I've heard about people who have read self-development books and panicked that they weren't going through the exercises quickly enough or that it wouldn't work if they didn't read it all in one sitting. Some people worry that they can only fit in a chapter a week or that there is a right or wrong way of following the process. If there are times when the process seems tough, realize that you are totally in control and can speed up, slow down or change direction as you wish. The power tool in Life DIY is you and the more action you take, the more powerful you become.

☐ **I'm in control of my life**

DO YOU HAVE PLANNING PERMISSION?

If you haven't experienced it directly, I'm sure you've heard stories of how someone's home improvements can affect others - early morning drilling, blocked views, devalued property, messy skips on the road and mismatched extensions.

As you begin to work on yourself, those around you will be affected - friends, family, partners, work colleagues, in fact anyone who has any kind of relationship with you. Change always has a ripple effect. It is a potent force and those close to you may feel that they're being left behind. I encourage you to be prepared for the effect your own change will have on those around you and to elicit their support (see Dream Team below). By sharing with your nearest and dearest you're making a further commitment as well. And your DIY can have a positive and powerful effect on the lives of others too.

☐ **I'm mindful of those around me**

CHECK YOUR BUDGET

To buy paint you first have to calculate the surface area you want to cover, to buy flooring you need to know dimensions. Many a home stands half-finished due to lack of time, energy and funds, and sometimes this is due to unrealistic miscalculations.

Whilst there is little financial cost to DIYing your life, there will be an investment of time and energy and you want to have sufficient to complete the project. You're probably wondering how you'll know how much that is? Well, there's no way of predicting exact quantities. So what I'm really asking you is: are you committed to making yourself a priority?

Decide now that you will allocate time and energy to yourself. You're in control of exactly how long you take to complete your improvements, but if you're going to do something, you might as well do it properly!

☐ **I give myself time and energy**

BRING ON THE DREAM TEAM

How would you like it if a Dream Team came into your home and within 24 hours you had a totally revamped house, complete with a Japanese garden and water features?

Many people think that taking the easy option means getting someone else to do the hard work for them. Actually, this sounds like the easy option, but when strangers are let loose on people's homes, they often end up with something which disappoints or even repulses them. That's why I want you to take the phrase 'DIY' literally. There has been enough outside influence on your life to date, so it's time for you to take control. The dictionary says DIY is 'the activity of making or repairing things yourself, instead of buying things ready-made or paying a workman to do the work for you'. Of course, this book is here to support you and guide you in the right direction - rather like the sales advisor in the home improvements store. As part of your Dream Team, I will guide you. I will be honest with you about my own experiences. I will help you as best I can through any sticky times and entertain you where possible! But with any personal change, you have to do it yourself because you know best what you want. Only you can change yourself.

☐ **I take responsibility for my own changes**

LET'S GO!

Client Case Study

I was at a conference in America where the speaker, having talked for a while about motivation and making changes in your life, shouted out to the audience, 'Let's go!' The group had reached such a level of collective frenzy and energy that amidst whoops and cries of 'Where?', 'Great!' and 'Right on' some people started to get up to take action.

I decided to repeat this stunt at one of my seminars in the UK to see what response I'd get. Having roused my audience for an hour, I shouted out, 'Let's go!' No one showed any sign of moving. I could hear the low murmurs of 'What's he on?' 'Don't be ridiculous!' and 'I can't do that.' And that's not because I don't have a charismatic presenting style! It just showed a difference in the collective way of thinking. As is often the case with British audiences, this group was swathed in cynicism and apathy, and whilst there may have been some 'Let's go!' kind of people there, the magnetic pull of the cynics was enough to dampen the sparks of excitement.

I don't want you just to be sitting there. I want you to be as passionate as I am, about you making your life better. On a cry of 'Let's go!' I want you to think, 'Great ! Where do we start?' or 'Thought you'd never ask!'

So, are you just going through the motions or are you really going to go for it?

☐ **I'm enthusiastic!**

HAPPY BIRTHDAY

Do you remember your birthday as a child, how exciting it was to be faced with a pile of brightly wrapped presents or to close your eyes and feel wonderful mystery gifts being placed in your hands? Some of you may still get this feeling now! I want you to turn the pages of this workbook with the same excitement with which you unwrap special gifts.

You may get bubbles of anticipation when you think of chipping away at the layers of paint that are hiding your real self, though there may be a few little tugs of fear as well. There is a very fine line between fear and excitement: in fact, for many people, the two emotions feel physically the same. Our interpretation of them is what labels them and affects our experiences. So whilst you may feel a little wary of the unknown, acknowledge the excitement and anticipation as well!

☐ **I'm excited about making discoveries**

ROVING EYE

I want you to be observant, to look back at things that happened in your past and at things that are happening to you now. You probably already do this, but it's the viewpoint you take that I'm interested in. Most people only look at things through their own eyes and become critical rather than step back and take a different view.

When you take a step back from a situation you are involved in, you can detach yourself from any emotions and see things from a different viewpoint. The case studies and snapshots in this workbook will help you to see things from a distance and learn even more.

Become more open in your views - you never know what you might see!

☐ **I'm flexible in the way I see things**

TAKE IT EASY

How often do you hear someone talk about something 'bad' that they've done or about what a 'good' week they've had? 'Oh, no dessert for me, thanks. I'm being good!' or 'I'm dying for a drink – my day was so bad!'.

I encourage people not to get too involved in labelling things as 'good' or 'bad' and not to be so judgemental. When you're judgemental about the things you do, it affects the way you feel. When I take people through the Life DIY process, I strongly suggest that they are gentler and more patient with themselves and just learn from what they've done, rather than judge themselves.

☐ **I am easy on myself**

CHOICE IS FUNDAMENTAL

Snapshot

Jane had asked her son Thomas to do the washing up three times already and he was still sitting in front of the TV. Each time she asked, she got more irate and could feel her blood pressure rising. Thomas had expected to do the washing up all along, as it was usually his job, but he just wanted to finish watching his favourite programme first. The more his mum nagged, the more he felt like digging his heels in and the more he ignored her. His motivation to help was dwindling rapidly.

When Thomas felt he was exercising personal choice, he was prepared to wash up. As soon as he felt that he was being controlled, the little rebel in him took over and resisted the pressure. Similarly, it's important for you to do the exercises in this workbook whilst retaining your power and freedom of choice. Every step of the way you can choose whether to read on, whether to re-read, whether to skip a section or whether to disregard what I say. Choose to DIY your life in your own way!

☐ **I'm choosing to change**

PERCEPTION IS PROJECTION

This is a concept that underlies many different schools of self-development and therapy. It's an idea that can be traced back to the roots of ancient religions, such as Buddhism, that instruct you to change yourself first, rather than trying to change someone else.

Client Case Study

Alison came to see me because whenever she spent time with her father-in-law she felt tense and the conversation was often stilted. Because she usually found it very easy to get on with people, she assumed that her father-in-law was uncomfortable with her and wondered what his problem was.

With my help, she admitted that she felt uncomfortable with her father-in-law because she believed he was always sizing her up and that he didn't feel she fitted in with the rest of the family. Once the idea that her perception of his discomfort with her was probably a projection of her own lack of comfort with him (and herself), she decided to change her approach and act as if she deserved a place at the family table.

'It was as if I was talking to a different person,' she told me later. 'The tension lifted and we both seemed so much more relaxed. This makes every family gathering something to enjoy and look forward to.'

Alison had realised how much simpler it is to change your own behaviour, than battle to change someone else.

Remember that your actions, words, emotions and even mere presence have far-reaching effects on all those around you. All change starts with you.

☐ I'm focusing on myself

WAIT FOR THE PAINT TO DRY

One common question people ask when they're embarking on personal change is 'How long will it take?' This is rather like waiting for the ideal property to come along - who knows? I won't give you guidelines as to how long to spend reading each section of this workbook or working on an exercise, as everyone works at different speeds. You may be the kind of person who wants to read the workbook through before revisiting each part thoroughly or you may want to dive straight into the exercises as they come along. I don't mind, so long as you give them a go!

Some people take time to find their dream home and once they've moved in, will live in it for a while and get a feel for the place, before they start knocking down walls. They have a clear image of what they want and take their time to complete their task. When they paint anything that needs more than one coat, they wait for each layer to dry before applying the next one and before touching it. Others paint something only to rush and touch it before it's dry and end up regretting the subsequent mess and smudges. Some people are so impatient with life that they even rush through reading personal development books, so that they can tick another one off the list without taking the time to do the exercises fully and to gain the most they can from them. Just because you've got the T-shirt doesn't mean you've been there.

Whatever your style, I want you to get the most you can from this experience. So take time to absorb what's here and give the exercises your full attention. And be patient with yourself! Some changes can happen almost instantaneously, but others require drying and setting time. To coin a phrase, Rome wasn't built in a day.

☐ **I'm patient with myself**

GET OUT OF YOUR HEAD!

How many people spend more time thinking about doing something than actually doing it? These people belong to the 'Do It tomorrow' school of never actually getting anything done. It's often easy to delude yourself that you're making progress by writing plans, having ideas and chewing the metaphorical fat. But DIY is about doing; that's why it's called "Do It Yourself" and not "Think about It for a Long Time and Never Do It At All."

Just reading this book may elicit some change, but it's living this book that will make the real difference. If you aren't prepared to do this (or aren't prepared to do this right now), put the book aside for a while or give it to someone you know who has a burning desire to change.

Many people let a barrage of opportunities pass them by because they don't believe they can make the most of them or because they require effort. But what's the point of an opportunity if you don't take it?

I have worked with many people who want to achieve change. I can help them to change their beliefs, I can help them to be more motivated and

I can give them huge amounts of information. But the people who are most successful are those who 'get out of their heads' and actually build on the work we've done together. So once you are clear about what you want to do, stop thinking about it and take action!

☐ **I act on my thoughts and discoveries**

WORDS THAT CHANGE LIVES

The majority of people don't say particularly positive things about themselves. The kinds of things I often hear my clients say are 'I'm so stupid, I can't get anything right' and 'I never seem to do the right thing.' No wonder it's difficult if you talk to yourself like this all the time!

Look back over the affirmations you've ticked. Instead of putting yourself down with negative statements, you can use these as a reminder of your commitment and drive. Research shows that affirmations can influence our health and sense of well-being – and they're great motivating tools too!

Here's a checklist to make sure you've got all the tools you need. Read these affirmations through again out loud and notice which ones make you feel strong and positive. If any of them feel strange or difficult to say, it's usually an indication that this is an area of your life that you need to work on.

TOOLS CHECKLIST

☐ I'm going to be honest with myself.

☐ I'm in control of my life.

☐ I'm mindful of those around me.

☐ I give myself time and energy.

☐ I take responsibility for my own changes.

☐ I am enthusiastic!

☐ I'm excited about making discoveries.

☐ I'm flexible in the way I see things.

☐ I am easy on myself.

☐ I'm choosing to change.

☐ I'm focusing on myself.

☐ I'm patient with myself.

☐ I act on my thoughts and discoveries.

Quick Fix

Choose the three affirmations that you know will be the biggest support to you. Write them on post-it notes and put them in places where you will see them a lot. The more you say them, the more you'll start to believe them.

Chapter 2
Interior Design

Imagine you wanted to do some work around the home and you met an interior designer, builder or architect to discuss the options open to you. They would look to work with you to achieve what you wanted, skip around any potential difficulties and start as soon as possible. Both of you would have a pretty clear picture of what you were aiming for and would be aware of the benefits it would bring.

In the same way, in order to get really psyched up for change in your life, you need an idea of what you want and what the benefits will be - maybe higher self-esteem, a more positive outlook or a head that's free of worries. And then you need to act.

> **Vision without action is a daydream. Action without vision is a nightmare.**
>
> Japanese Proverb

Sounds simple, doesn't it? But isn't it often the case that you know something needs fixing around the house - a coat hook that keeps falling off, a corner of the carpet that trips you up, a table that wobbles whenever you put anything on it - yet for some reason it's left undone for a long time? You know that if you did it, your life would be easier - you could hang up your coat securely, walk around your living-room without stumbling or put down your cup of tea without it spilling over - and you wonder why you keep putting it off. Why can't you just get on with the job? Does this sound familiar?

> **Even if you're on the right track, you'll get run over if you just sit there.**
>
> Will Rogers

So why are so many people plagued with the procrastination bug? They put off going to the dentist, getting their eyes checked, doing their tax return or tackling the ironing. Have you ever put off doing anything like this? Well, a very common reason is that your brain tells you that the job is going to be hard work. It rifles (consciously or not) through memories of when jobs were banal and full of hassles and didn't work out. So you decide that not doing anything is the way to avoid boredom or failure.

When I was a personal trainer I could never understand why so many people would join a gym and then spend all their time avoiding going. All these people had a very effective way of talking themselves out of exercising: they would make images of being sweaty, self-conscious, uncomfortable and even bored. A Life DIY technique that I always used to motivate these people was to focus on what was in it for them. I got them to make pictures of being full of energy, fit and healthy and having fun. They imagined the feeling they'd have at the end of the session – the glow, buzz and satisfaction - and I encouraged them to exercise with those feelings in mind. They could either talk themselves into exercise or talk themselves out of it: the choice was theirs. It's the same for you.

Quick Fix

Think of something that you need to get done that you've been putting off for a while. Maybe it's clearing out a cupboard, writing a letter to someone or making a phone call. Imagine what you'll get out of doing it. Picture yourself having done the job. What do you feel like? Think about the satisfaction, sense of achievement and relief of having done it, until you can really imagine what it will be like.

Take the feelings you've imagined and do the job itself, keeping those feelings with you as you do, and then notice how you feel afterwards.

Most people want something to work towards, something to draw them in, a purpose for their efforts. One of the most widely used management techniques is to give incentives to employees - recognition, remuneration, time off, opportunities and promotions. When the right carrot is dangled, most people will go for the bite. The real key to change is giving yourself incentives. That is what this step is all about.

A mission could be defined as an image of a desired state that you want to get to. Once fully seen, it will inspire you to act, feel your motivation and determine your behaviour.

Charles Garfield

HOW HUNGRY ARE YOU?

Challenge

PART ONE

Take a moment to think about the things that you want to achieve from going through this workbook. Here is the list of bonuses I mentioned earlier. You may have your own to add too.

- to be happier
- to have more confidence
- to feel more positive about life
- to break unwanted habits
- to have better relationships
- to feel healthier
- to realize your full potential
- to feel better about yourself

Choose three things that you want the most at this stage. I know that there may be more but just choose three for this exercise.

1. ....

....

2. ....

....

3. ....

....

PART TWO

Now let's rate your desire for these three things using a scale of 1-100, with 0 being the minimum and 100 being the maximum:

How much do you want these things?

....

....

....

....

How motivated are you to do something about them now and to keep working at them?

....

....

....

....

What do you notice about your answers? Are the scores the same or is one higher than the other?

....

....

....

....

If your first score is higher than your second one then you're in the very common position of wanting something more than you're motivated to work for it. This is quite normal, believe me! What we need to do now is redress the balance so that you're up for persevering until you get what you want. The good news is that with a highly motivated attitude, you can achieve things more quickly and enjoy the process as well!

WHAT GETS YOU GOING?

> *There's real magic in enthusiasm. It spells the difference between mediocrity and accomplishment.*
>
> Norman Vincent Peale

Motivation is feeling determined to achieve something and being prepared to work to get it. It's really a very simple idea, but many people think that the world is divided into two types of people, the Motivated and the Unmotivated. But the fact is that everyone is motivated to do the things that they enjoy doing - for example, if you enjoy watching TV, you do it; if you enjoy eating junk food, you do it!

Client Case Study

Brian booked a session with me because he wanted to stop smoking and get healthier. His girlfriend was pregnant and he wanted to be 'clean' for when the baby arrived. We established that if he looked into his future he could see a very unhealthy, wheezy man who couldn't run around with his children and that was enough for him to decide to change. But he insisted that he wasn't a motivated person. He claimed he was lazy and had always been this way.

I challenged Brian to find things he was really motivated to do. At first he didn't grasp what I was getting at, so I helped him out. I found a whole list of things that he was motivated about: smoking a lot, watching TV, procrastinating, believing how hard it was to change, drinking and cultivating a hefty gut!

Challenge

Write down a list of things that you're motivated to do, that you put a lot of time into and that take up a lot of your energy and effort. It's not a question of what's 'right' or 'wrong' or 'good' or 'bad', but rather things that you put a lot of time and effort into.

Look at this list and think about how good you are at doing these things - even if some of them don't do you any good. Are you prepared to channel some or all of this determination into more nourishing pastimes?

What motivated you to buy this home study programme? Was it the joy of having a better life or was it because there's something that you want to change?

From my experience, what finally gets people to change is a build-up of discomfort and sometimes even pain. Some people can live with a small pile of ironing or paperwork, but will actually do something about it when the pile is huge. Those who are overweight usually experience a certain amount of physical and mental discomfort before they change and, on a more extreme level, some people have to be faced with serious illness, like a heart attack, to be motivated to alter their harmful habits.

There are a number of motivation strategies and the most common one is moving away from what you don't want, like the examples I've just given.

The other key motivation method, which I've already mentioned, is focusing on what you do want and thinking about how much you want it and all the benefits you'll get from having it. I want you to have both kinds of motivation running, so that you are really driven to DIY your life.

WHAT'S IN YOUR WAY?

I'm always doing things I can't do, that's how I get to do them.

Pablo Picasso

When people want to change, the things that often stop them from doing so are their mental comfort zones. For many it's the fear of the unknown or of failure; it could be that they believe that the way they are is the way they're meant to be; it could be anger that they've left it so long and a feeling that they've left it too late. It's ironic that sometimes a lot of the things that hold people back are the ones they want to get rid of. Is this true for you?

I want you to realize what powerful resources you have in your quest for change. We all have them; we just use them in different ways. If you harnessed all the determination and drive you have and re-directed this energy to make the changes you want, you'd be a force to be reckoned with!

CHRISTMAS IS COMING

Do you know Dickens' story 'A Christmas Carol'? Scrooge spends his life hanging onto his wealth rather than sharing what he has with others and enjoying his life. He continues to live this way until the Spirit of Christmas Future shows him what his life will be like if he carries on. He takes a look at himself becoming more miserable and lonely until he breaks down in tears and can't take any more. His life was bearable in the present, but to see it in his future and 10 times worse, was too much for him to handle. He's finally prepared to change.

> **Do not let the future be held hostage by the past.**
>
> Neal A. Maxwell

One of the most powerful techniques I use to help people change, is to get them to focus on the consequences of their actions if they carry on living the way they have been. The next challenge will encourage you to do this. It should help crank up your motivation and get you to pick up those DIY tools and get to work.

Challenge

There are two parts to this challenge and it's important that you do the second straight after the first. You'll need between five and ten minutes to do the complete challenge, so make sure you leave yourself enough time. You may want someone to read it out to you or you can record the instructions onto a cassette to play back.

PART ONE

1. Sit comfortably. You may have your eyes open or closed, whichever you prefer.

2. Take a moment to consider what would happen to you if you continued living your life the way you have been, at the mercy of your negative thoughts and emotions.

3. Imagine being in front of a full-length mirror in eight weeks' time. What do you see when you look at yourself? What do you feel about yourself? What does your life look like? What do you hear people saying to you? What are you saying to yourself? Use all your senses to imagine this. Notice the feelings you get from carrying on this way.

4. Now imagine arriving in front of the mirror in six months time, having dragged with you the behaviour and emotions that you no longer want. Feel how they are getting heavier and holding you back.

5. Now travel one year from now, still with everything that you no longer want. As you look in the mirror again, see how much more pain you feel when you look at your life. What do you notice? How do you feel about yourself? What sounds do you hear now?

6. Project your life five years into the future, still hauling with you all the uneasiness that you associate with your current behaviour. What is your life like now? How are you feeling as you think about it? How do you think you'll feel then?

7. Now take the consequences of your actions even further into the future. Go 20 years into your life and consider what your behaviour will be like then, when your habits and comfort zones are firmly established. What do you see and hear and feel?

8. Ask yourself if this is the person you want to be in 20 years' time.

9. Stop your daydream and slowly bring your attention back to wherever you are.

Now here comes the good news: none of this has happened! Feel relieved that you imagined it all. Be grateful that it was make-believe. This is not what will be, but what could be.

If you still feel you are not ready to change, go back and repeat this before you move on to Part Two. If you feel more motivated now, then move on.

PART TWO

This part of the exercise is much more uplifting!

1. Sit comfortably.

2. Think about DIYing your life and the changes that you want to achieve.

3. Imagine being in front of a mirror in eight weeks' time. You've become more positive and feel better about yourself. Imagine how good you look and how great you feel as you look at your reflection. Use all your senses to make your image clearer, brighter and bolder.

4. Notice the feeling you get from behaving in a different way and take that pleasure six months into the future. You're acting like the person you want to be and have left behind the behaviour and emotions that you no longer want. Imagine seeing yourself in the mirror again and feel how free and energised you are.

5. Now travel one year from now, still continuing this new way of living. As you've broken your patterns of behaviour for a whole year, see how much more excited you feel when you look at your life. What do you notice? What sounds do you hear? What are people saying to you?

6. Project your life five years into the future, when the new you feels like second nature. What is your life like now? How are you feeling as you are thinking about it and how do you think you'll feel then? What are you saying to yourself?

7. Now take the results of your change even further into the future. Go 20 years into your life and consider what it will be like when your new habits are firmly established. What do you see and hear and feel? What emotions are taking you over now?

8. Ask yourself if this is the person you want to be in 20 years'time.

9. Stop your daydream and slowly bring your attention back to wherever you are.

Now, here comes even better news: this is what can be and you can start to move towards this now!

Repeat this daydream every time you feel you need a motivation boost - or even just for fun!

We often DIY when something has got out of control and we can't take it any more - when the damp is so bad that it affects our breathing, when the rot has set in so much that the floors are unsafe, when the wobbly door handle finally packs in and we get stuck in the house. But when we nip things in the bud, they are much more manageable and quicker to sort out. If we tighten a screw when it becomes loose, we are saving ourselves work in the future. If we weed the flowerbeds regularly, it's a small task compared to taming and pruning a jungle.

Don't wait for life to become more difficult. Decide now to change your life for the better.

One to Watch .

SCROOGE
The movie adaptation of Charles Dickens' A Christmas Carol. If you get the chance to watch this, it will increase your motivation.

MOVING BEYOND THE LIMITS

If you don't know where you are going, you might wind up someplace else.

Yogi Berra

Have you ever embarked on a project without having a clue about what you wanted to do? Aimlessness can make life very difficult and wastes time and energy. I would hazard a guess that both your time and energy are precious to you, so it's important that you use them wisely.

Have you ever thought about some of the greatest construction projects ever: the Pyramids, the Great Wall of China, St Mark's cathedral, the Eiffel Tower? All of these started with a vision - even if it seemed impossible at the time.

What is impossible? In 1961 the barriers of possibility moved as the first man went into space. Prior to 1954 very few people believed that man could run a four-minute mile. So why was it that once Roger Bannister broke the four-minute barrier, a stream of other runners did it too? Was there a sudden shift in human running ability? Or was there a shift in the mental barrier that had blocked everyone until then? What do you think will happen once the two-hour marathon barrier has been broken? I bet there'll be a spate of new 'miracle' runners.

We're geared to limit ourselves to what we're told we can or can't achieve and we are also affected by how much others believe in us. A study was undertaken once to prove that the way pupils are treated by teachers affects their academic results. The teachers were told, before meeting the pupils, who the brightest ones were, even though, on past track record, this actually wasn't the case. These formerly average performers then went on to outperform their classmates because of the way they were treated. They were treated like stars and so performed like stars!

Scientists have done a fantastic job of learning about our bodies and minds, yet despite all their efforts they admit they only understand a tiny fraction of how the human body functions and the potential it has. So what does this mean? It means that we really have no idea how capable we are or what we can achieve.

So many of us spend so much of our lives exposing ourselves to negativity: dire newspaper stories, depressing television shows and soap operas and people who drag us down. What we don't realize is that by focusing on mediocrity and negativity, we're limiting our potential. In order for us to DIY our lives effectively we have to focus more on what we are capable of, rather than being transfixed on what's wrong and what's missing and what we can't do. Start to look beyond these false limitations and see what's really out there for the taking.

Quick Fix

The next time you find yourself unnecessarily reading or watching or talking about something depressing, STOP!

Find something to do that will lift your spirits and change your mood.

Write the following affirmation on a post-it note and put it in a prominent place.

Affirmation

Every thought I think is shaping my future.

DARE TO DREAM

If you ask young children what they want to be when they grow up, those who say 'pop star', 'actor', 'actress', 'dancer', 'footballer', 'gymnast', 'president' or 'prime minister' really believe that it can happen, because to them, there are no limitations. Speak to them 20 years later and they will probably have abandoned their dream, because it would have been too hard. It wouldn't have been a 'proper' job or they simply wouldn't have been good enough to do it.

Some children will say they want to be a doctor, nurse, teacher or firefighter. Again, 20 years down the line, many of them will have weighed up the long working hours, poor pay, staff shortages and lack of recognition and plumped for seemingly easier options.

As we grow older, we may realize that what we once wanted is not really right for us. Maybe we wanted to be a tightrope walker just because our best friend did or we wanted to be a doctor because we came from a medical family, but on closer inspection we saw that those lives just weren't for us. But some of us still have unfulfilled ambitions.

One thing I've noticed since I started writing books, is how many people have admitted to me that they have always wanted to write a book or that they began writing one many moons ago. They all have a dream but aren't following it. How many people do you know who have songs half-written, degrees unfinished, business ideas that have got no further than the back of a beer mat? What have you always wanted to do? What's sitting on your back burner? Write three down in the space below. They don't have to be ground breaking.

I have always wanted to...

....

....

....

....

Quick Fix

Imagine how you would feel if you had accomplished any of the things you have listed above. Keep this feeling of achievement with you as you read on.

At first, dreams seem impossible, then improbable, and eventually inevitable.

Christopher Reeve

GOING FURTHER

> *People who say it cannot be done should not interrupt those who are doing it.*
>
> Retep Nehoc

When we were younger, we used to give things a go and open our minds to new experiences, even if we weren't going to be world champions. So why do most of us stop dreaming? Why do even more of us lose the belief that we can and will follow those dreams?

We don't actually lose our ability to dream, we just alienate ourselves from it. Often teachers will tell us not to daydream and there comes a time when we feel silly for having 'unrealistic' expectations. We start to think that the celebrities and record-breakers we see on TV are superhumans, who live in a different world.

Yet the fact is we can all go further and we can all do more, especially when we become more aware of our limitless potential.

Challenge

1. Stand up and imagine you're in the middle of a clock face, facing the number 12. Point your dominant arm straight out in front of you.

2. Keeping your feet facing 12 o'clock, move your arm around your body as if it were moving around the dial of the clock. See how far around you can go and mark the spot.

3. Come back to where you started.

4. Now put your arm out in front of you again and, keeping it totally still, just imagine doing what you've just done. See your arm going further and further around the dial. Even imagine it moving full circle.

5. Now actually move your arm round again.

See how much further you can go when you've imagined it first and broken through the limits! This exercise demonstrates that our brains put limitations on us but that when we imagine going further, we can break down these barriers and achieve greater things.

FOCUS ON YOUR DREAMS

Now that you've started to think about how your life can change, I want you to think even more about what you can achieve. Like all great designers and creators, you need a clear vision of what you're working towards.

So go back to the three things you wrote down earlier, those three dreams you had. What would happen if you made a simple choice to start these things? I'm sure you've all heard that you get what you focus on. Well, it's time to make that focus really clear.

> **Visions expand the horizon; the greater the vision, the greater the goal that will be achieved.**
>
> Will Carling

CROSS THE THRESHOLD

There is a very old tradition of a groom carrying his new bride over the threshold of their marital home. This symbolizes the end of their separate lives and their new beginning together. To signify the end of your old ways and the start of your new behaviour, I want you to imagine crossing your own threshold into the future.

Challenge

1. Take a new page in your Life DIY notebook and write down how you want to be once you've made your changes. Go into as much detail as you can. The clearer your vision, the more likely you'll be pleased with the finished result.

2. Pay attention to the following:

   • how you will look

   • the expression you will have on your face

   • the feelings you'll have

   • the sensations in your body

   • what you'll hear yourself saying

   • what you'll hear others saying to you

   • what you'll be doing

3. Take as long as you need to perfect this. Enjoy the process of planning.

4. When you've done this, think of a door that you have good associations with, maybe your own front door, or make one up.

5. Stand up and imagine that on the other side of that door there is the new you, just as you've described, with all the physical and mental qualities that you want.

6. Picture the new you standing about a foot in front of you, with its back to you and the threshold between you.

7. Imagine seeing that image turn around. See that future you from every angle - from the back, sides and front. Make the picture as clear and colourful as you can. Make the sounds you hear more distinct. Notice how you start to feel.

8. When you're facing the back of that image again, take a step over the threshold into your future and try it on for size.

9. Allow yourself to feel all the things you imagined and make those feelings as powerful and enticing as you can. Think about all the things that you're leaving behind on the other side of the threshold and notice the feeling of lightness and liberation. Close the door on your old behaviour.

10. When you've let those good feelings sink in, slowly bring your attention back to your surroundings, bringing that new you back into the here and now.

Do this exercise again and again. I recommend that you do this at least once a day or that you repeat it whenever you want to be reminded of how good you can feel.

When you change, you're just taking on a different role and playing a different part. This is how actors and actresses play diverse characters - by living and breathing their lives. See how long you can keep acting in your new way. But don't worry, because it's not your opening night! You don't have to play the part perfectly straightaway. Life DIY is about trial and error and you're always rehearsing and learning how to do things better.

> *I have missed more than 9,000 shots in my career. I have lost almost 300 games. On occasion I have been entrusted with taking the game's winning shot and missed. And I have failed over and over again in my life. And that is why I succeed.*
>
> Michael Jordan

One to Watch

DEAD POETS' SOCIETY
Watch this film if you want to see the power of following your dreams and to understand how important it is to seize the day.

Chapter 3:
Make Your House a Happy Home

Quick Fix

Imagine how you would feel if you had accomplished any of the things you have listed above. Keep this feeling of achievement with you as you read on.

a) Throw your toys out of the cot and take out your anger on the steering wheel?

b) Scream and shout at the cars moving freely in the opposite direction?

c) Smile at a neighbouring driver, plan how you can rearrange your day and take the extra time to collect your thoughts?

The answer is pretty irrelevant. What is relevant for you is to recognize that you have a choice. Almost every situation in life is a multiple-choice of reactions and emotions and only you can choose the answer. An uneducated monkey is supposed to be able to score over 50 per cent on multiple-choice tests just by random answering, so surely we can do better than that. Yet sadly, a lot of people don't realize that they have a choice at all and allow themselves to be victims of circumstance.

> *Everything can be taken from a man but one thing; the last of the human freedoms - to choose one's attitude in any given set of circumstances, to choose one's way.*
>
> Victor E. Frankl

When you choose how you react and therefore the direction of Your life, you are more likely to achieve happiness and fulfilment. But how to gain happiness? Well, it doesn't come in a pill (despite what some people may lead you to believe) and it can't be bought (despite wishful thinking). So how can you make yours a happy home?

WHAT MAKES US HAPPY?

> *The purpose of our lives is to be happy.*
>
> The Dalai Lama

Convincer

A study by the University of California at Irvine and the Loma Linda (CA) University School of Medicine showed that people who viewed a one-hour humorous video experienced a decrease in stress hormones in the body, that lasted between 12 and 24 hours. Even anticipating something funny can help lower stress levels.

With the help of clinical psychologist Dr Carol Rothwell, I recently conducted some research into happiness for Thomsons, a well-known holiday company. Our remit was to pinpoint what it is that makes us happy and to look into the effects of holidays and sunny weather on the human psyche. We collected vast amounts of information from numerous studies that had been done on happiness all over the world and the culmination of our findings was an equation that allowed people to calculate their happiness levels.

When the results of our study were published, it caused a media frenzy in 22 countries and my radio and television interviews were broadcast in places as widespread as America, Argentina, Australia, Canada and Korea. This makes me think that people are definitely looking for an answer to happiness.

Before I tell you more about how you can calculate your own happiness, answer this. Of the following two men, who do you think would be happier: a single multi-millionaire with a yacht, sports cars and houses all over the world but no roots, no need to work and a high turnover of short-lived romantic liaisons, or a man with a moderate income, a loving wife, two children, a successful career in a solid company, good health and a close family network?

Well, according to multiple psychological studies, including our own, it is highly likely that the latter man will be happier, despite his relative lack of material wealth, because he has a loving stable family network and a sense of purpose. Why is this? Well, as we become wealthier, in material terms, our expectations adjust and so do our aspirations. It's not material wealth that makes us happy, but how close we think we are to meeting the standards we've set for ourselves.

This point is well exemplified by big lottery winners. They are said to experience increases in happiness for a couple of years until their baseline of aspirations is locked into a whole new league. The trappings of wealth, which their win initially brought them, are soon considered the norm and they want more. Whilst they were once happy with a semi-detached house, now they want a mansion complete with heli-pad.

> *Success is not the key to happiness. Happiness is the key to success. If you love what you are doing, you will be successful.*
>
> Herman Cain

HEALTH WEALTH

Almost everyone, regardless of their bank balance, has at some point considered themselves to be 'broke' or 'strapped for cash'. But what do we really mean by that?

All of us have basic needs of food, shelter and clothing. Lack of these, along with social and racial inequality, political unrest and coercion and poor access to meaningful education, are critical factors in defining levels of happiness. These are our existence needs, They are the basic ingredients that have to be there before any icing can go on the cake and it's the person who can't meet these who is truly justified in claiming 'broke' status. This does back up the idea that whilst money can't buy happiness, it can make unhappiness a lot more bearable!

So, if the mere presence of a happy meal and a few happy-hour drinks is not enough to guarantee a blissful life, what else do we require? Well, with these basic foundations in place, we can exercise certain social, economic and spiritual choices (higher order needs) that further raise our level of happiness. Examples include having a sense of purpose, security in who we are and emotional support at our fingertips. And I guess this is where our two hypothetical characters differ: both men have the basics of food, shelter and clothing, but their circumstances add a very different finish, and in this case, fancier is not always better.

Just as quick hits, like lottery wins, don't have long-term happiness benefits, so the effects of traumatic events (for example loss of sight. hearing or mobility) only lead to a short-term drop in well-being. This suggests that we all have a set point of happiness that we tend towards. Some studies argue that this set point is genetically determined and others claim that we can change it. I would say that each and everyone of us has the ability to choose to see life through rose tinted glasses or cracked and smudgy lenses. This allows you to shift your set point to increase your chances of enjoying life, regardless of what you have.

It was this information that gave Carol and me the basis for our Happiness Equation.

The Happiness Equation

happiness = personal characteristics + existence needs + higher order needs

To summarize each part of the equation:

Personal Characteristics

These can be inherited or learned, In part they define how we relate to other people, face challenges and adapt. To a certain degree they can be unlearned and relearned and I'll talk about this idea throughout this workbook. It has been proven that people who are more outgoing, energetic, optimistic, resilient and flexible will also tend to be happier. Our research suggests that these personal characteristics account for approximately 20 per cent of our overall levels of happiness.

Existence Needs

Once you have the basic roof over your head and crust of bread. the most important of these basic needs are health, financial security, personal safety, a sense of belonging and engaging in meaningful activities,

Higher Order Needs

These relate to a deeper outlook on life and personal relationships. Self-esteem, challenges, meeting expectations, depth of relationships and intensity of experience are all critical factors. Once our basic needs have been met, our levels of happiness become a reflection of the choices we make, the friendships we form and our emerging comfort with ourselves, Just indulge me and read that last sentence one more time!

Your Happiness Quotient

> *Happiness grows at our own firesides, and is not to be picked in strangers' gardens.*
>
> Douglas Jerrold

I know that happiness is a subjective emotion and that some people may be cynical about how you can quantify such an intangible, but what the following questionnaire does is give you an idea of how happy you are relative to how happy you can be. It also helps to pinpoint where you need to focus your attention. It's a quick and easy barometer that you can use to see how changing certain factors in your life can make a difference. Remember it's a measure of your state of mind at a point in time and whilst your external circumstances may not vary, different moods will greatly affect the result you get.

There are four sections to the questionnaire:

Q1 and Q2 relate to personal characteristics

Q3 to existence needs

Q4 to higher order needs

To find out how happy you are, read each of the four statements and circle the number on the scale which you feel reflects most accurately the way you are at this point in your life. Enter the four ratings into the equation and complete the calculation. It's simple, honestly!

HAPPINESS QUOTIENT (HQ) QUESTIONNAIRE

Self Assessment
(circle the number which best describes you)

Q1. Personal Traits: To what extent do you see yourself as someone who is outgoing, energetic, flexible and open to change?

Not at all   **To a large extent**

0   1   2   3   4   5   6   7   8   9   10

Q2. Outlook on life: To what extent do you see yourself as someone who takes a positive outlook on life, bounces back quickly from setbacks, feels that you, and not fate, is driving your life?

Not at all   **To a large extent**

0   1   2   3   4   5   6   7   8   9   10

Q3. (circle the number which best describes you)

Basic existence needs: To what extent do you feel your basic needs in life are met in relation to personal health, financial subsistence, personal safety, freedom of choice, sense of community/ belonging and, access to education/knowledge?

Definitely not met   **Definitely met**

0   1   2   3   4   5   6   7   8   9   10

Q4. (circle the number which best describes you)

Higher-order happiness needs:

To what extent are you currently able to:

- Call on the support of people close to you?

- Immerse yourself in what you're doing?

- Meet your expectations?

- Engage in meaningful activities that give you a sense of purpose?

- Feel a clear sense of what you are and what you're about?

0   1   2   3   4   5   6   7   8   9   10

Happiness Quotient (Results)

Happiness = Personal Traits & Outlook + (5 x Existence Needs)

+ (3 x Higher-order Needs)

Your score:

Happiness = Q1 + Q2 + [5 x Q3] + [3 x Q4]

THE STRENGTH OF FOUNDATIONS

Our research has shown that there is an important dynamic relationship between the basic existence needs and higher order needs. By meeting the existence needs, a platform is provided on which to build feelings of self-esteem, intensity of experience, and so on. For example, if someone with all the required personal characteristics and outlook on life had met all of their higher order needs, i.e had fantastic self-esteem, support and a sense of purpose (a score of 10/10 on Q4), but had no home or food to eat, thus scoring low on the existence needs (2/10 on Q3), our research would suggest that they'd be significantly less happy than the person who had met all their basic needs (10/10 on Q3), but needed to do some work on their higher order needs (2/10 on Q4) - overall, 60 per cent versus 76 per cent happy.

If you don't have the basics in life, you can attempt to add all the frills you like. But you should not overlook addressing these foundation needs - after all, who would build a house on shaky ground?

HOW DOES THIS TIE IN TO LIFE DIY?

When you Life DIY, your existence needs are more likely to be fulfilled if they aren't already. For example, you are more likely to motivate yourself to sort out your living arrangements, if you feel you deserve to. You are more likely to raise your earning potential and therefore financial security if you have more confidence and your health will probably improve once you shed the weight of negative emotions. But what this process will really address are your personal traits, your outlook on life and your higher order needs.

Just put your answers to one side now as we move on to step 4. We will come back to them later.

Also put this affirmation somewhere where you will see it at least once a day.

Affirmation

I love life.

One to Watch

PATCH ADAMS

Watch this film to see how much of a difference being happy and having fun can make to your health and well-being.

Chapter 4
Building on Solid Foundations

When you came out of the womb, how would you describe yourself? Let's see... Small, helpless, inquisitive, in touch with your body's needs, open to love, flexible, outgoing, energetic, gentle, adaptable, non-judgemental, free of prejudice and expectation: clean and pure like fresh white walls. According to the Happiness Equation, the personal traits that are likely to give you the most happiness are all similar to the qualities with which you were born.

Did you know that the human species is one of the few which give birth to very helpless babies? The young of other animals often rely on their parents for food and protection for a short while, but soon, if not immediately after birth, they are able to walk, fly or swim and fend for themselves. Human babies, however, learn to walk on average at 12 months of age Our basic needs, like feeding and cleaning ourselves, take years for us to fulfil on our own and some people are still emotionally dependent on their parents way into adulthood.

Another dependency we have is financial dependence. Many of us rely on our parents for money until we are fully educated and, on the whole, the more developed the society, the longer this reliance lasts. Children in developing countries are taught to fend for themselves at a much younger age.

I'm certainly not claiming here that parents stunt their children's potential in order to wield the mighty sword of influence for a few more years. Neither does this book address the nature vs nurture issue. Whilst predispositions to some emotions discussed here can arguably be inherited, please remember that what I'm writing about is the effect of conditioning on our behaviour.

What do you think are the differences between the way you were as a young child and the way you are now. It's as if you started life in a spotless new home. Then clutter crept in. Have you ever noticed how suddenly you can be faced with a mountain of things that need clearing and you don't even know how they got there? Only by understanding where the clutter came from can we learn what use, if any, it has for us and then we can start to sort out what we want to keep and what needs to go.

> **The big thing is not what happens to us in life, but what we do about what happens to us.**
>
> George Allen

CURIOUS AND OUTGOING

Snapshot

Bobby has just discovered the freedom that crawling brings; he can dart around the house poking into all the corners that he has previously been kept away from. One day he approaches the oven with anticipation, drawn by the tantalizing smells emanating from it. One touch of the door, a split-second reaction time and several decibels of screams later, it becomes clear to him why he was kept at a distance. He has just learned something as a result of his curiosity.

As very young children we asked questions, we were outgoing in the sense of wanting to reach out to touch things, we pulled things apart and threw things to see if they would bounce. We made discoveries because we dared to be curious. And then what happened? We were told that curiosity killed the cat. Sticking your nose in where it didn't belong would just get you into trouble. Formal learning was less focused on discovery and more on listening and absorbing. Even science experiments were often rigged for the desired and most time-efficient outcome.

Learning as a young child was like a journey of adventure; there was room for the discovery of new and unexpected places, tastes and people. However, as we get older our learning can become more like a package holiday where the whole foreign experience is brought to us rather than us going to find it for ourselves.

Just as we'll probably never have time to visit every place in the world, so we'll never know everything. But that doesn't mean that we can't regain the curiosity we used to have, especially about what makes us tick.

> **He who asks a question is a fool for a minute; he who does not remains a fool forever.**
>
> Chinese Proverb

ADVENTUROUS AND ENERGETIC

As toddlers, our lives were one big adventure. Bathtime was a sea voyage, bedtime was an exciting journey to another land and playtime was anything you wanted it to be. Even mealtimes could become an escapade with aeroplanes of mashed potato and swamps of tomato ketchup. We just did things for the fun of it and for the sheer joy of doing.

But chances are you were told: 'Stop playing with your food', 'If you're going to splash around, you're getting straight out of the bath! ', 'Grow up and stop being silly - you're not really Wonder Woman.' There comes a time when those repeated messages dampen our adventurous spirit. We're encouraged to give up our thirst for excitement and adopt a sensible 'grown-up' life that, quite frankly, can seem staid and boring.

Yet life can continue to be an adventure, if you want it to, to the day you die. If you allow yourself to rekindle the exploratory nature that we all have, life can become much more fun!

If you approached life as an adventure more of the time, what do you think you would achieve?

Quick Fix

Remember some of the adventures you used to have as a child. Take yourself back to some of those moments and experience again the excitement you felt at the time. Notice how that feeling can get stronger the more you focus on the experience. Plan to do something adventurous soon!

FULL OF LOVE

Babies are like little love bundles waiting to swap love with other human beings. They beam out unconditional love and are open to receiving it back because they are free of experiences that lead them to rationalize it. As we get older, we still feel the desire to give and receive love and we all have the capacity to do so. But many of us change from being open to giving and receiving love to becoming afraid of doing so. What happens to make us afraid of loving? When do we start feeling afraid of being hurt? What makes us conscious of the fact that we become vulnerable? What makes us vulnerable at all?

As children we readily tell those close to us that we love them and yet when we're older those three little words are some of the most frightening ones to utter. What will happen if our love is thrown back in our face? Very few of us love ourselves and we fear rejection. If someone doesn't tell us we're loved then does that make us worthless? There is a common misconception that if someone else loves you then you'll automatically love yourself, but, as I'm sure you're aware, it's not as easy as that.

Quick Fix

Do something to show someone you love them and don't expect anything in return.

Maybe you've been dying to tell someone that you love them and you haven't had the guts. Do it today!

HAPPY AND CONTENTED

Happiness is an emotion that isn't reliant on anything or anyone; it's a state that arises within us rather like an endorphin rush. When we were young, before we were aware of possessions, people or results affecting our mood, we would experience bursts of unprompted joy. I like to think of this spontaneous elation as getting high on our own supply.

As we go through life however, we become increasingly dependent on external factors to be happy. Think back to a time when you felt happy. Was it because of a compliment, a new car, success at work or your team winning? Now can you think of a time when you felt happy and you can't remember why? What gave you that joy?

Pure joy isn't usually reliant on anything but the conclusion many people have come to - that happiness is brought about by things. And this renders it a fragile emotion over which we don't have total control.

We think of it as something tangible and therefore gained through tangible means. We are 'happy because. What about being happy for no reason other than being alive?

Quick Fix

Think about the things that make you happy. If they were all taken from you today, but you still had yourself, could you still be joyous about being alive?

FLEXIBLE AND OPEN TO CHANGE

As young children, we thought life was full of possibilities. Every corner held a potentially new experience and we took on all that was offered to us. We accepted those who were different from us and we opened up to new things without prejudice or judgement. Like sponges we soaked up new tastes, sights, smells, sounds and feelings. We have just as much potential for new experiences at any stage in our life, yet we often close ourselves off to them for no good reason.

When I was a child my family would go to Chinese restaurants and I would take with me a McDonald's meal. I had never even tried oriental food, but had got the idea into my head that I didn't like it. I can't believe this now, because Chinese food is my favourite. I can't believe I missed out on so many delicious meals!

We would probably give most things in life a go if we never exposed ourselves to others' opinions or never adopted someone else's outlook in order to look sophisticated or knowledgeable. Imagine having no limiting judgements. What do you think you would have let yourself experience if you had always been completely open?

Quick Fix

Next time someone says something you don't agree with, listen to what they have to say without judging. See if you can learn something new - even if it doesn't change your viewpoint.

FREE-SPIRITED

Each one of us is born an individual, unsullied by the influence of other people or of life itself. As youngsters we connect with others whilst sustaining our sense of identity. But there is a great contradiction in human nature. Most of us want to keep our individuality but also want to be accepted and feel as if we belong to society. Take the example of fashion: we want our clothes to express facets of our own personality, yet we choose them according to what appears in the fashion pages or on the catwalks.

There are some key stages in life, when we go through significant change, when we are caught between the lure of being one of the crowd and of having our own identity: puberty, late twenties/ early thirties, the mid-life milestone marked by turning 40 and retirement. These are all times when we tend to question what path we're on and assess our achievements to date. Also, because of the transitory nature of these periods, we feel stuck sometimes between two identities and often hesitate about making the rite of passage.

Just as a solid is made of atoms which all move randomly, so we can belong to the "solidity" called society whilst still remaining an individual atom. But to do so we have to throw out the style catalogues and make a home for ourselves that is truly unique. It's often all too easy to give in and become just another empty show house.

Quick Fix

Write a list of the things that you've only done to follow the crowd. Maybe you tried drugs when you didn't want to. Maybe you went to a party when you wanted to stay at home. Perhaps you bought a fashionable car despite the crippling monthly payments. Think how different your life would be if you hadn't done these things and had just done what you wanted to do.

PRESENT

Snapshot

Remember little Bobby and the incident with the oven? His mother picked him up, comforted him and distracted him from the pain with his favourite mobile of dangling dinosaurs. Like the sun creeping out from behind a cloud, a smile crept over Bobby's face. Once his attention had been diverted from his tingling hand, he let the pain go. Bobby is a master of his own state. He moves easily from pain to pleasure.

As babies we all had this ability to really experience an emotion and then move on. We controlled our moods rather than letting our moods control us. Time is of little consequence to young children. They focus on what they're doing or feeling at every moment and then allow it to pass, readily accepting the next.

As adults, we can be aware of our moods for hours, maybe even days, holding onto them to gain attention, sympathy or as an excuse for being miserable. It's easier for us to wallow in a state for too long, focusing on what was or what may be, rather than paying attention to what is, and so we ruin the present moment.

Quick Fix

When you next have an emotion that isn't energizing or nurturing, time how long you have it for! What else could you have done with that time? Bear this in mind, as I will be building on this later.

RESILIENT

When we learned to walk we fell down all the time and just picked ourselves back up. We carried on going because we didn't take our stumbles as personal attacks. We wanted to walk and so we kept trying, regardless of how bruised our bottoms were. When we started to feed ourselves we spilt food everywhere, but we didn't storm away from the table, ranting that we'd just give up and starve. At what point did we come to believe that giving up was going to get us anywhere?

As children we didn't claim that it was fate determining we remain on all fours or that some higher power had decided that we weren't to eat that day. We didn't use fate as an excuse for our failings or setbacks; we took control of what we wanted to do and got on with it.

Many of the worthwhile things in life require hard work and resilience; there are times when things don't go the way you'd like them to and then you have choices: give up, do the same thing again or find a way around the block.

> **A man may fail many times, but he isn't a
> failure until he begins to blame somebody else.**
>
> John Burroughs

**JUST BECAUSE THERE'S NO GLITTER DOESN'T MEAN
IT'S NOT GOLD.**

Snapshot

In 1957 a group of monks in Thailand had
to relocate a large clay Buddha from their
temple to a new location to make room for
a new highway to Bangkok. It began to rain
and the head monk decided to cover the
sacred Buddha with a large canvas to protect
it. Later that evening he went to check on it,
shining his torch under the canvas to see if
the Buddha was still dry. He noticed a gleam
catch the light and wondered whether there
might be something under the clay. Using a
chisel and hammer, he started to chip it away.

As he knocked off shards of clay, the gleam
grew brighter and brighter. Hours later, the monk
was standing face to face with an extraordinary
solid-gold Buddha that measured 10 feet tall
and weighed over two-and-a-half tonnes.

Experts believe that several hundred years
earlier when the Burmese army was about to
invade Thailand, the monks of the time had
covered their precious golden Buddha with a
coating of clay to protect it.

Many of us are like the Buddha, with our treasures covered to protect us from the world. But we can all shine. We haven't lost any of the gifts I've talked about in this chapter; it's just that many of us have lost sight of them. We all have the gifts that can bring us happiness. So let's start digging for gold!

Affirmation

I am willing to change.

One to Watch

AS GOOD AS IT GETS

Watch this film for an insight into how much better life can be when you let go of your mental comfort zones.

Chapter 5
Contents Valuation

So, your house may be built on firm foundations, but who's living in it?

I heard the other day that Elvis Presley entered an Elvis impersonator competition. He came fourth and gave the winner tickets to see him perform in Las Vegas! It's OK to aspire to certain aspects of another person, but I've never understood the desire to become another person. I think there's a lot of truth in the saying 'You're better off being a first-class version of yourself than a second-class version of someone else'.

Snapshot

When I was in college, my psychology lecturer asked us to write on a piece of paper who we most wanted to be and to give three reasons why. I wrote down:

Pete Cohen
Loving, caring, good bloke

I think a lot of people thought that what I wrote was a joke, but I didn't want to be anyone else. Even though I was aware of my insecurities, I just wanted to be myself. I was ridiculed for it, but my lecturer pinned up the piece of paper in the middle of the wall.

Somewhere along the way a shift takes place in us. Babies are congratulated on anything they do well, even the most natural bodily functions. Then later the confidence that's been built up starts to be knocked down. Our society often ridicules positive behaviour because we're brought up to think that nobody should think a lot of themselves and so the act of putting ourselves down can become a habit.

> *If you want your children to improve, let them overhear the nice things you say about them to others.*
>
> Haim Ginott

DANCE TO YOUR OWN RHYTHM

The award-winning film Billy Elliot tells the story of a young boy growing up in the north east of England during the early 1980s. His father and older brother are miners who are struggling through the strike. Billy wants to be a ballet dancer more than anything else in the world and has to hide this from his family, but inevitably they find out that he's been skiving his boxing classes to go to ballet lessons. His father is furious that his son wants to dance: dancing is only for poofs! He values being like other men, whilst Billy values his dream. And so the battle ensues between father and son.

It would be easy for Billy to follow in his father's and brother's footsteps and mimic what a 'real man' should do and be. Instead he chooses the rockier path that his instinct tells him is right for him.

As we follow Billy on his difficult route it's hard not to wonder what the world would be like if we all followed our heart's desires. There would be no measure of whether we were 'good enough': we'd just be the way we were meant to be.

Quick Fix

Take a new page in your Life DIY notebook and write down three reasons why you want to be yourself. Think about what qualities you have that you really value.

Start to appreciate who you are now.

One to Watch
BILLY ELLIOT
If you want to feel inspired about following your dreams, then Billy Elliot is one to watch!

VALUES: HAVE YOU INVESTED WELL?

If you had an investment portfolio of stocks that had done well for a number of years but then some of them started to decline, what would you do? You might decide to sell off those that were starting to devalue and maybe reinvest in others, depending on the markets, or you may keep hold of them all for old time's sake and just in case they regained their former value.

The values we have as children are usually love, fun, freedom and security. We invest in different values and beliefs as we get older. The values most of us invest in are the ones that our parents want for us, usually stability and security in the form of money and love. What comprises stability for most people in the Western world is a sound job and steady relationship. I'm not saying that this is wrong, but sometimes the emphasis on these things is too great and OUR own personal value falls by the wayside.

Let's look closer at the values of work and love that many of us hold dear at the expense of our own true value.

WHISTLE WHILE YOU WORK

For many, Wednesday lunchtime around the water cooler is like reaching stalemate in a tug-of-war - being equidistant from either previous or future weekends results in inertia and frustration. How many people really enjoy their jobs?

Some people put up with unfulfilling jobs to achieve wealth and all that comes with it. What often happens, though, is that if you pursue money too much, you don't allow yourself the time to enjoy it.

We often select our careers according to what we think we should be doing to match our academic achievements, earning capabilities and peer group. Careers guidance is dished out to fulfil these needs too and, in the case of schools and universities, also to guarantee impressive alumni.

Sometimes circumstances have to be thrust upon us for us to make decisions that allow us to follow our real desires. There have been a lot of redundancies of late in our economy. The whole of an IT department in a large investment bank was laid off and I looked at what some of the individuals went on to do. One opened a bookshop in a coastal town, one retrained as a cabinet-maker, one travelled around the world. Sometimes we'll only jump if we're pushed. What would people say if we left respectable, safe and successful jobs to go against the grain and take risks?

Still, values are changing now to make it acceptable to admit you want more out of your career and to do something about it. Recently there has been an increase in demand for career coaching and books on how to find your true calling in life. They all talk about finding what you really enjoy and believe in, which is great advice. Why not start to think about it?

> **It's a very funny thing about life; if you refuse to accept anything but the best, you very often get it.**
>
> W. Somerset Maugham

OWN HAIR, OWN TEETH

As I said earlier on, we are programmed to want to connect with other people, but I also believe that we want to retain our independence at the same time. Yet those who like to spend a lot of time on their own are often considered to be emotional cripples.

Society is becoming much more supportive of the single person, but there are still pockets of it which expect and value an 'other half' culture, regardless of what the whole is really worth. Being alone and being lonely are often confused. A popular form of punishment for children is to set them apart from the group or to send them to their room and the worst thing that can happen in the playground is being sent to Coventry. If you argue with your partner, chances are one of you will be banished to sleep on the sofa or in the spare room. In prison, misdemeanours are punished with solitary confinement. We're given messages from a young age that it's not normal to be alone and that there must be something wrong with you if you're sitting at a table for one.

Anyone still single at a certain age has their sexuality or their ability to commit queried. Or you're thought of as just too plain fussy and should set your sights a little lower. After all, what's wrong with someone having a little extra baggage, a few spare toes or a little extra body hair? But what may actually be true is that these singletons (self-confessed or not) value themselves so highly that they are waiting for the right match to set their house on fire.

Affirmation

I am worth loving.

Another way in which the values we collect around relationships affect us, are our reactions to a relationship that starts to go wrong. Maybe your moment together has passed and it's time to move on or maybe your moment was over a long time ago but you have to hold on to the burning coal for a long time to be convinced that it's actually burning your hand. Perhaps stability is such a core value for you that you'd rather be in a stable loveless relationship than risk upsetting the applecart to get something better.

When it comes to affairs of the heart we're not given clear guidance. It's like painting a room - there are no fixed colour rules but you have to choose something you can live with. The decisions we take usually depend on the family, religion, culture and how we were brought up.

Some people believe that if you leave a relationship, particularly where children are involved, you're selfish, whereas for others, if you stay, you're stupid and gutless. It may be better for the children if you stay and complete the nuclear family or it may be unhealthy and damaging for them to witness discord between their parents. All relationships have challenging times and you can often pull through them, but how do you know when you've overstayed your welcome?

If you always care about what society expects you to do, you'll find it hard to make the right decision. You're damned if you do and damned if you don't. There will always be arguments for and arguments against and too many people listen to the argument that's put across loudest rather than to what their gut instinct tells them. The fact is the more you start to value yourself, the quicker you get what is right for you. That is the heart of Life DIY.

> **You have no control over what the other guy does. You only have control over what you do.**
>
> J. Kitt

EXPECTATIONS: HOW LONG IS A PIECE OF STRING?

So how long is a piece of string? It's a hard question to answer. Isn't It? It depends on so many factors it's not even worth going into. And this is a common response to many questions. When will I meet my soul mate? When will I feel happy with myself? When will I be successful? All of these things are hard to quantify and we all have different benchmarks.

Benchmarks and comparisons are introduced to us early on in our lives. We probably all remember marks out of 10 on school tests; critics mark music, books, films and restaurants out of 10; consumer magazines compare food, drink, white goods, cosmetics and a host of other products, all on a scale of 10; work promotions and bonuses are often decided on performance measures out of 10; and some people even rate how attractive they find members of the opposite sex out of 10 (although they'd probably never admit it!). A lot of us compare ourselves to external criteria and our comparisons leave us feeling substandard.

It's no wonder that most of us carry a belief of not being good enough: not good enough at our jobs, not good enough in relationships, not good enough as a mother/father/daughter/son. Again, the list is endless.

> **The best inspiration is not to outdo others but to outdo ourselves.**
>
> Anonymous

The benchmarks we use define the degree to which we feel the pressure of meeting expectations. Many people feel pressure to fit in with the right look and to lead a certain lifestyle when it's not at all feasible or when they don't even want to, but they fail to question what they do really want. A lot of the time we are comparing apples and pears but we feel comfortable measuring ourselves against others, rather than just viewing ourselves as we are.

Snapshot

Jenny was a sporty girl with an athletic body. She had taken after her father, who was naturally strong with well developed muscles. Her older sister Mary had inherited their mother's petite build. Jenny had spent her wonder years copying her older sister's behaviour and for the most part she modelled her effectively and formed a sound character in doing so.

But unconsciously, Jenny had also taken on board the idea that physically she should be like her sister and mother and this belief was exacerbated by copious images of waif-like models in the media. So Jenny assumed that to be an attractive and successful woman you had to be thin.

Nobody's saying that this is rational, but we can see how this belief came about; Jenny didn't know any different. And so she began to diet, thinking that this was an easy solution to the problem. She'd then be thin enough to be the sort of woman she aspired to be. But she was trying to fit her foot into a glass slipper that was just too small.

Affirmation

I let go of all expectations.

HOW MUCH IS ENOUGH?

How can you judge what's enough or what's right for you? Enough food for an elite athlete is probably far too much for a sedentary office worker; someone else's treasures are another person's clutter. We may all inhabit one planet but we all live in very different worlds and this extends further than the differences between Mars and Venus.

Expectations, benchmarks and rating systems have led almost all of us to believe that we're not good enough in some realm or other - not clever enough, not confident enough, not interesting enough, not attractive enough, not thin enough or just simply not good enough. What often happens is that we let this belief ripple out to contaminate all areas of our lives. Remember Joe, who wanted a nose job?

YOUR UNIQUE PATCHWORK

So we can see that as we've grown up we've sewn together a patchwork of lots of people's values and expectations, and taken on board their opinions and beliefs often without questioning whether they serve us in a positive way. A lot of what we've taken on from others forms the moral foundation of who we are. But some of it may no longer be of use to us.

The next two exercises can be a chance for you to thank the people who've influenced you with positive outlooks and opinions, as they're probably unaware of the gifts they've bestowed. And you can also look at those booby prizes you've picked up - the beliefs and values that stop you from being your true self.

Challenge

Draw a table in your notebook and write in each box the name of someone who has been influential in your life.

Put your own name in the middle and leave room to write more!

Mother	Father	Brother/Sister
Peers	Me	Grandparents
Peers	Best Friend	Mentor/ Teacher

2. Under each name, write down what traits you've picked up from these people - both positive and negative.

3. Answer the following questions:

If there is anything here that you no longer need/want? Can you live your life without them? Can you give up this behaviour?

....

....

....

....

What things have you done in your life to please other people? Do you think you're being someone else's you, not your own?

....

....

....

....

If you were living your life again, what would you choose to leave behind? What would you make sure you kept hold of?

....

....

....

....

Once you've established to what extent you're living someone else's values, you can decide whether they serve you well or not.

Remember that some of the ideas and values you have from others do work well, so there's no need to completely rebuild your house. You're just sorting through your attic and throwing out the old things that you no longer need. You don't have to make room for anyone else's old junk. Instead, you can start to choose what you have in your life. By choosing your own beliefs and expectations, you will value yourself that much more and can make your life easier and more enjoyable.

> *Be more concerned with your character than your reputation, because your character is who you really are, while your reputation is merely what others think you are.*
>
> John Wooden

GET OUT OF YOUR BOX

The last exercise will have helped you to sort out who has had an influence in your life, both positive and negative, and the traits that you've picked up throughout. But what I want you to keep in mind is that we are all much more than the total of those traits.

It's often too easy to label yourself according to your behaviour. I have heard many clients say: 'I'm a smoker', 'I'm a terrible mother', 'I'm a jealous person', 'I'm a fat person', 'I'm a doormat.'

How would you describe yourself?

- 'I'm a happy person.'
- 'I'm a sad person.'
- 'I'm a stressed person.'
- 'I'm a worried person.'
- 'I'm a negative person.'
- 'I'm an unconfident person.'

- 'I'm an angry person.'
- 'I'm an excited person.'
- 'I'm an adventurous person.'

Client case study

Jerry came to see me complaining that he wasn't a confident person. He insisted that he lacked confidence the whole time and that it was ruining his life. Even if he could pretend that he was confident in certain situations, he knew it wasn't true and tortured himself about how he should be able to cope the way he saw other people do. On talking to Jerry it was apparent that he did lack confidence in his abilities at work and that he also got quite overwhelmed at big parties.

I sat Jerry down, put a piece of paper and a pen in front of him and asked him to write down all the things in his life that he did with confidence. The paper stayed blank. I waited for a while as Jerry got increasingly uncomfortable: he couldn't believe he was even failing at this task and felt even more like a loser.

The aim of the exercise was not to make Jerry feel worse about himself; it was actually to make him realize how much of his time he spent feeling confident. So I started him off with a few pointers. Together we soon saw that Jerry was confident when he drove, when he was with his family, in small gatherings, on a hockey pitch, on a squash court, when he cooked for friends, when he was walking his dog and when he was doing bits of DIY around his house. Even at work, there were certain parts of his job that he felt very confident doing. So we managed to distil the times Jerry did lack confidence down to when he was taking on new jobs, when he was with one particular colleague and when he was at big parties where he didn't know many people.

Given the total time these activities took up in his life, it was apparent that Jerry was a confident person for about 80 per cent of the time and was unsure of himself for about 20 per cent of his total waking hours. How much better do you think he felt when he realised this? How much more confident did he automatically feel at work, regardless of what he was doing?

From the dark confines of his box, Jerry couldn't see how much of his time he spent feeling confident. The more he focused on his lack of confidence, the more it became an issue. I helped Jerry to step outside his box, look at this life objectively and to remove the label he had given himself.

Like many of us, Jerry found it too easy to focus on the things that he wasn't happy with and transferred the feelings and beliefs he had about these to every other area of his life, until he'd totally tarred him self with the brush of no confidence. He had become alien to his capabilities and to who he was put on this Earth to be.

PERFECT 10

In Frank L. Baum's family film The Wizard of Oz, when the Wizard is revealed as being a dupe, he defends himself from the onslaught on his whole character by saying 'I'm a good man, I'm just a very bad wizard.'

We all play different roles in our lives and lots of people's self-worth is determined by how well they think they perform these roles. An exercise I do to help people value themselves more is to get people to write down all the roles they have in their life, for example husband, wife, carer, daughter, employee, employer, mother, auntie, driver, cleaner, cook, lover, friend and entertainer.

I then ask them to give themselves a mark out of 10 for each role, compared to the best that they can do, given their ability. Next, I ask them to put all of these roles to one side and to rate themselves as a person, regardless of what they do.

I've seen plenty of people give themselves a variety of marks for their various roles and when they come to mark themselves, they never give themselves full marks.

In my opinion, everyone is a 10, regardless of how well they play their roles, and we need to move away from the idea that our worth is determined by these stand-alone actions. They don't seem standalone because we feel so defined by our roles and because they take up so much of our life. But there is more to everyone of us than the roles we play.

One of the key ideas in the Life DIY process is that you came into this world as a 10 out of 10 and you still are, regardless of what has happened to you.

Challenge

1. Take a clean page in your Life DIY notebook and draw a circle in the middle of it and lots of other circles around it. Leave room to write a couple of words in each.

2. Write 'Me' in the middle circle and then jot down in each of the other circles a different role you play. Use the list of examples above for ideas.

3. Now mark out of 10 how you think you perform each role. Remember to compare yourself only to the best that you think you can be - not to anyone else!

4. Now give a mark to yourself as a person and write it in the middle circle. It doesn't matter if you don't see yourself now as a perfect 10, as this book will help you to do that. Just see how great a person you are, regardless of what you do.

Whatever score you gave yourself, it's time to recognize your true worth: you are a perfect 10. You always have been and you always will be.

Affirmation

I am perfect as I am

One to Watch

AMERICAN BEAUTY

Just watch this film!

Convincer

To help you to appreciate how amazing you are, I've put together a list of 10 facts about you. Read them through and marvel at how awe-inspiring you really are.

1. In one hour, your heart works hard enough to produce the equivalent energy to raise almost 1 ton of weight 1 yard off the ground.

2. Put all the blood vessels in your body end to end and they'd stretch about twice round the world!

3. There are 300 million air sacs in your lungs that provide oxygen to the 100 trillion cells in your body.

4. You breathe 15-18 times per minute, more than 7 million times per year and about 500 million times in a lifetime.

5. Fifty thousand of the cells in your body will die and be replaced with new cells, while you have been reading this sentence.

6. You eat 1100lb of food each year, which is about the weight of a small car!

7. In a year, your heart beats about 40,000,000 times.

8. About 400 gallons of blood flow through your kidneys in one day.

9. You have 206 bones and 656 muscles, forming a system of capabilities that is more functionally diverse than that of any known creature.

10. And finally, you are totally unique: there is nobody else like you in the whole world! You are amazing beyond belief!

Chapte 6
Rewiring

What part of your body sends messages at 240 mph?

What part of your body generates more electrical impulses in a single day than all the world's telephones put together?

Which part of your body has over 1,000,000,000,000,000 connections - more than the number of stars in the universe?

Which part of your body is made up of 15 billion cells?

The answer to all of these questions is your brain. Your brain is your body's power tool. Many people believe in the power of computers but the brain is more complicated than any computer we can imagine: the world's most sophisticated computer is currently only as complicated as a rat's brain.

The brain controls everything in the body: it processes a vast quantity of information about what is happening around us and inside us. It's the decision-maker that issues instructions to the rest of the body. Crucial messages pass in and out of the brain through a network of millions of nerve cells that pass on information to other nerve cells, rather like a very complex electrical circuit. The brain is also responsible for regulating our emotions and our bodily sensations such as pain, thirst and hunger And, as if it didn't have enough to do, it also takes care of memory and learning.

Scientists believed until recently that, unlike the other organs in the body, the brain was not capable of renewal or growth once we had attained adulthood. This view is now changing, due to evidence to suggest that new brain cells can be produced throughout the whole of our lives.

In 1998, researchers working under the direction of Professor Fred H Gage at the Salk Institute of Biological Studies in California and at the Sahlgrenska University Hospital in Goteborg, Sweden, discovered that large numbers of new brain cells develop in an area of the brain involved with learning and memory. Research is continuing around the world to corroborate these findings and to establish whether other regions of the brain behave in the same way. So far the results look very encouraging and the data suggest that learning stimulates the development of new brain cells, which reinforces the 'use it or lose it' theory of brain ageing.

All this is still very new and a great deal of work still needs to be done, but the findings increase the likelihood that our experiences throughout adulthood can actually alter the structure of the brain. Now it seems possible that the development of new circuitry in the brain may also play a role in memory. Researchers are emphasizing that we still do not know for sure what these new cells do, but it looks as though we may have more control over our own brains than we thought.

This is, of course, great news for anyone who wants to change some of their own thought patterns or forms of behaviour. It suggests that we do not have to remain victims of the way we are made. This naturally does not include medical conditions; they always require expert medical examinations and treatment. But for everyday activities, it appears as though we might actually have the capacity to change the circuitry in our brains by changing our behaviour or the way we think.

> **What happens is not as important as how you react to what happens.**
>
> Thaddeus Golas

THE MIND/BODY CONNECTION

Your body follows what your mind tells it to do. Every time you repeat a thought, you reinforce it. The circuit or pathway along which you think gets stronger and because the brain is so powerful, if you engage it in negative emotions like worry, stress or anxiety, it learns to perform these emotions very effectively. On the other hand, your brain can also be used to create and reinforce powerful connections for positive emotions. You can rewire your brain.

Wiring is very important, whether it's in a house or the brain. It's fundamental, we take it for granted and it's vital that we sort it out before any of the other DIY work can be undertaken. Good wiring in both cases lasts a long time, keeps us safe and gives us the power to function well without having to think about it. Poor wiring can lead to explosions and breakdowns.

Snapshot

James had just bought a newspaper and a can of cold drink. The sun was charging him with an energy and buzz that he hadn't felt in ages. He loved the laziness of Saturday mornings which allowed him to walk at a relaxed pace rather than his usual frantic dash. He turned the corner into the road where he'd parked his car, diverted by the tanned legs of a young woman. He had been able to take the top down on his car for the first time this year and as he approached it, he admired its waxy blue exterior. Life was sweet! He settled himself into the driver's seat and got ready to cruise past the lovely legs.

Then he spotted it. It was about to ruin his perfect day. It was the thing that annoyed James more than anything else. It was small yet significant and it was an all too regular occurrence in James's life. It was a parking ticket.

James felt a rush of heat shoot from his stomach to his head, hotter than any charge from the sun, and with it came an intense anger that made his fists clench and his temples throb. The sun's rays became annoyingly intense, the headline on the newspaper turned depressing and the lovely legs were long gone.

When different sensations come into the mind at the same time, even seemingly unrelated ones, the brain links them together. So James had such an intense reaction to his parking ticket because his brain had automatically associated parking tickets with feelings of anger.

We have spent our lives building up connections between certain things with certain feelings so, if someone extends a hand toward us we tend to shake it; if we hear sirens, we think of trouble; when the bell rings at school, we start to pack up our books; when we see a red traffic light, we stop (most of the time); certain voices can make us switch off or turn us on; a look from a loved one can make us feel warm inside; a threatening hand hovering over a ticklish child invokes giggles; a parking ticket can bring anger in an instant. We are always going in and out of different states or moods and these often come from the way we link things with emotions.

That is not to say that everything triggers a strong response, as we take in billions of pieces of sensory information each second. Shortly I will talk about what makes some stimuli significant whilst others pass us by.

Snapshot

Jimmy was visiting a friend for lunch. He parked his car on a meter and as the two friends hadn't seen each other in a while, they didn't notice when the two-hour parking limit expired.

Suddenly realizing the time, Jimmy popped his head out of the window to see if he could spot a ticket on his windscreen. The sight below was potentially much more infuriating. There was a parking warden in the very process of putting a ticket on his windscreen!

Rather than get het up and ruin a great afternoon, Jimmy shouted down to the warden (who was, after all, just doing his job): 'Hi! That's my car! Can you just move the ticket a bit over to the left, please?'

The warden was completely flummoxed but once he realised he wasn't going to be bombarded with the usual verbal abuse, he smiled up at the window, waved and moved the ticket! Once that was sorted, Jimmy settled in to finish his lunch - after all, the worst had already happened.

In both cases the parking ticket was inevitable - as anyone who has contested one will know only too well. In situations like these, where one person is at fault, if you accept the consequences and move on, you need not get stressed. James let the ticket ruin the rest of his day and Jimmy let it go. A switch was turned on in both these men but the message that came down the wire was very different.

> **A healthy attitude is contagious, but don't wait to catch it from others. Be a carrier.**
>
> Shaggy Mumford

The wiring we have in our brains to react in certain ways is key to how we live our lives. There are many things you do or think, that are hard-wired in your mind and some of these are really useful to your day-to-day existence.

Quick Fix

Tick the things that you do automatically:

☐ Brush your teeth

☐ Wash your hands when you've been to the bathroom

☐ Drink when you're thirsty

☐ Say 'Bless you' when someone sneezes

☐ Change gear when you drive

☐ Say sorry if you bump into someone

☐ Laugh when something funny happens

☐ Shake hands when you meet someone new

Why do you do these things automatically? Well, because you once learned them and have practised them ever since. You went through a number of stages of learning and a good example of this is when you learned to drive. To start off with you were really quite clueless about the mechanics of driving but didn't realize this (what psychologists call the 'unconscious incompetence' stage); then after the first lesson it's quite likely that you became more aware but you still couldn't do it ('conscious incompetence'): after a few lessons you started to get the hang of it but you had to work hard at remembering what to do (the 'conscious competence' stage); finally, after a number of lessons, you started to drive without thinking about it. You'd reached the stage of 'unconscious competence', where your brain just did it for you automatically.

In the Life DIY process I don't want you to label the habits and emotions you don't want as 'bad', but rather to see them as things that you do because you've practised them until they've become automatic. With a little more practice you can replace them with healthier and happier habits.

Have you heard the phrase 'Practice makes perfect'? I prefer to say, 'Practice makes permanent. So make your practice perfect!' That way you'll practise the things you actually want rather than becoming an expert at draining yourself and getting what you don't want.

WHAT TRIPS YOUR SWITCH?

We all have certain habits or reactions to everyday situations that aren't really useful. What are the automatic reactions that you'd like to get rid of?

Challenge

PART ONE

Tick whether you have ever experienced these reactions and do add your own too.

☐ Queuing frustrates me.

☐ People who are late for appointments make me angry.

☐ When someone cuts me up I experience road rage.

☐ Delays on the road/public transport wind me up.

☐ Rejection makes me feel bad about myself

☐ Rude people annoy me.

☐ Criticism makes me feel depressed.

☐ Parking wardens get on my nerves.

Why do these things affect you? The answer is simple: you allow these things to get to you. You weren't born this way.

Now ask yourself the following questions about each statement in turn:

Am I choosing to behave this way?

....

....

Do I have a choice about how I react?

....

....

What does acting this way do for me?

....

....

What would be a more appropriate way for
me to behave?

....

....

You may think that you don't always choose how
you react, as your response is just too quick - how
could you decide so quickly to blow your top?
Well, chances are the first time you were in a
similar situation you chose to act that way and
(here's the bad news) the connection between
the event and your reaction became set in your
wiring and turned into an automatic response. But
here comes the good news: you can choose to
change your reaction.

The first step is to take ownership of how you feel. For example it's not traffic wardens who make you feel annoyed, it's you allowing traffic wardens to annoy you.

Challenge

PART TWO

I want you now to take each of the above statements you ticked, and any more of your own you wish to add, and change the way they are written so that you are the cause of your reaction. For example:

- I choose to let queues frustrate me.

- I decide to get annoyed by rude people.

- I allow criticism to depress me.

When you have written these out notice how you begin to feel about your behaviour: if you are the one causing it, then you are the one who can change it. You are in a position of control and power.

There is a third part to this exercise, which comes later, so just put this to one side for now.

LIKE A DOG WITH A BONE ...

Client case study

I was asked by one of the world's largest corporations to give a motivational talk to its UK sales division. I called the divisional head to ask him what he wanted to be the outcome of the talk. The reply was: 'I want each person to realize that they can make a difference.'

When I asked him what was currently stopping this, he said, 'Moaning, procrastinating, not taking pride in what they do, not feeling good enough and lack of confidence.'

I then asked him if he had any idea how much investment people had made in this behaviour. I said, 'If each person had £1 for each time they did any of these things, they'd all be rich, so why should they stop now? They feel that these things are part of them and life seems strange without them.'

If the head really wanted change to come about in the organization, he would have to encourage people to do things differently and so increase their self-worth and enjoyment in what they did.

Often people stubbornly resist change because of the time and effort they've put into being a particular way. They believe that because they have done something for a long time, that there's no other way. But there's always an alternative.

> *A ship in harbour is safe - but that is not what ships are for.*
>
> John A. Shedd

Challenge

Every time you do something to help yourself to change - be it doing a challenge, using affirmations, giving yourself credit for doing something differently - I want you to see it as a positive reinforcement of your commitment to DIY your life.

I want you to literally see the investment you're making in your own happiness and well-being. So get yourself a jar or tin and each time you invest in your future happiness, put a coin into it. See how positivity mounts up!

PLEASURE AND PAIN

Snapshots

Chris's father drank too much. He would drink himself into a stupor each evening and end up slumped in the armchair, snoring loudly and stinking of stale gin. Occasionally, he would surpass himself and actually manage to get up from his throne to hurl some abuse at his wife, sometimes at Chris and often at the cat. When Chris had friends over he would feel mortified by his father's embarrassing behaviour and would often get upset on his mother's account. Chris never touched a drop of alcohol in his life.

Shirley suffered angst at 17, as most people do. She would go to parties with her friends and feel like a complete wallflower as the boys bypassed her to flirt with her more confident friends. That was until she discovered the power of a few stiff drinks. She found that illicit drinking of fortified wine and sickly alcopops made her feel like a different person. She was more interesting, flirtatious and seemingly attractive. It worked every time. Shirley went on to become an alcoholic.

If any experience in our lives causes us enough pleasure or pain, we will make a connection between that situation and the resultant emotion. In Chris's case he associated so much pain with alcohol and its effects, that he formed the opinion that alcohol was disgusting and degrading. His brain linked a wire between alcohol and these emotions. Every time he was near alcohol, particularly gin, he would automatically think about his father and switch himself off from the social and pleasurable aspects that alcohol can offer.

Shirley, however, associated alcohol with confidence, feeling attractive and having a good time. Her brain wired a connection between booze and these great feelings, so every time she went to a party, or even if she just wanted to lift her mood, she turned to drink. Then she got herself into a downward spiral where she thought she needed her liquid crutch to cope with any situation, hence a daily alcohol habit.

What makes a stimulus significant enough to hard-wire a particular response in our brains? What such stimuli have in common, is that they tend to be linked to a considerable amount of pleasure or pain. Think about these different examples for a moment. Many people have a food that they just can't stomach. They will probably be able to link this disgust to a bout of food poisoning or with something they were told about that food. Most people also have a food that comforts them and gives them an instant hit of pleasure. This may be because it was given to them as a treat when they were young or maybe as a comforter when they fell over and cried. Perhaps they ate it at a time when they felt really happy or maybe they were always fed that food by a person they were very close to.

Often we don't even need to have experienced the pleasure or pain ourselves. Our brains are clever enough to react in this way with mere perceptions of the feelings.

Paula Radcliffe, the world-class British distance runner, is known for her intense training schedules and punishing ice baths following hard sessions and races. The thought of sitting in a bath of ice would be considered painful by most of us, but to Paula it means quicker recovery and ultimately a greater chance of winning and breaking records. She therefore associates enough pleasure with ice baths to be able to endure them willingly.

A novice exerciser, on the other hand, will often exercise to a point where they imagine pain will soon set in even though it doesn't. They aren't actually hurt, but perceive that exercise wouldn't be fun if it did start to hurt and so they stop just to be safe.

> **Ability is what you're capable of doing. Motivation determines what you do. Attitude determines how well you do it.**
>
> Lou Holtz

You may be wondering what associations you have. You may come to the conclusion that you don't have many. But we all have a lot of connections hard-wired in our brains. We're just unaware of them. When we boil the kettle, switch on the TV or turn on a light, we don't think about the electrical connections that make the water boil, EastEnders come on or the room light up. Similarly, we learn to expect reactions from ourselves and from others and take them for granted, not wondering what connections have made them happen and whether we can do anything about rewiring them.

BLOWING A FUSE

If one light bulb goes in your house, you can probably leave it for a while before you change it. I know someone who went three weeks without changing a bulb in her bedroom because she could survive using the light from her bedside lamp. But if all the lights blew, you'd probably do something about it pretty quickly. If someone told you that your electrics looked dangerous and could all blow at any moment, I bet you'd sort them out without delay.

We often have to be threatened by large amounts of pain to heave ourselves out of complacency. We are usually only prompted to look into how we're wired when we are in danger of being damaged by our own behaviour or have already totally blown up.

HOW DO WE REWIRE OUR HABITS?

Once you are ready to do some rewiring, the key to changing these automatic connections is to change the perception you have of pleasure or pain in your brain. It's not as complicated as it sounds!

Snapshots

Janet had been having an affair with Geoff for two years. She was single and he had a wife and two children. He had told her from the outset that he had no intention of leaving his family and just wanted a side order of fun. Janet believed deep down that eventually he would change his mind and want to be with her permanently and the pleasure of this thought kept her tied to the relationship.

One Sunday she was running in the park and spotted Geoff having a picnic with his family. She had never seen them together before.

They were laughing together as a unit - a unit of which she wasn't a part. The searing pain that cut through Janet brought her a new clarity: she realised that Geoff really wasn't going to leave his family and for the first time the pain she felt totally stifled any pleasant feelings she had. In that instant, her brain rewired itself to associate her affair with an intensely negative emotion.

Julie was a sociable sparky girl who knew how to have a good time. She would go out and have a few drinks and a few cigarettes. She had smoked on and off for about 10 years and had the association popular among smokers of 'fag in one hand, drink in the other, good night out'.

One day early in the New Year, following the usual bout of parties, Julie noticed a sharp pain in her left side. As the day went on the pain got increasingly worse, until coughing sent daggers of agony through her chest and she could barely stand up. She went to her local hospital and was told that she had contracted pneumonia in her left lung.

Julie was confined to bed for two weeks and was not well enough to work for another fortnight. Partying was out of the question – even walking to the corner shop left her fatigued and frustrated. Once she was well enough, she started to go out again and had as much spark as before, but she never touched another cigarette again. Her brain now associated cigarettes with 'fag in one hand, agony in lungs, serious damage to body'.

Both Janet and Julie's brains rewired themselves, practically without them choosing to do so; it's as if their self-preservation mechanism kicked in and saved them from long-term pain and damage. We can all make similar changes in our minds by consciously attaching pain to things that we want to cut ourselves off from and pleasure to the thought, action or object that we want to replace them with. You're probably wondering how you can do that...

Quick Fix

Make a quick list of all the things you've changed in your life. These may include:

- Hairstyles
- Clothes
- Friends
- Habits
- Words and phrases
- TV and radio programmes
- Jobs
- Homes

The reason you changed these things will probably be because you had something else to take their place. As the old saying goes, out with the old and in with the new.

These changes would have required some conscious effort initially but after a while they would have become automatic and felt normal. Let's see how quickly you can get comfortable with a change.

Quick Fix

- Fold your arms.
- Notice which way you automatically went.
- Now fold them the opposite way.
- How does this feel? Strange? Weird? Awkward?
- Now unfold and fold your arms, alternating your leading arm.
- Do this at least 30 times.
- How does it feel now to have your arms either way around? See how something different can feel more comfortable pretty soon.

ESTABLISH NEW CONNECTIONS

A nail is driven out by another nail. Habit is overcome by habit.

Desiderius Erasmus

Remember the exercise you started earlier? The one where you took responsibility for the emotions you felt? Shortly, you will be establishing some new connections around those situations. But before we do that, I want to tell you a story.

Snapshot

During the Second World War, a number of Japanese garrisons were sent to occupy little islands in the Pacific and were instructed to shoot at invaders or enemies of Japan. Because of their location, these garrisons had no radio contact with the outside world, so believed that the war was still going on long after it had ended. Some of these garrisons continued to don their uniforms, clean their weapons and shoot at passing 'enemy' ships well into the 1970s. It was thought that the gentlest way to break it to these men that the war was over was to send in a former sergeant in his old uniform to thank the men and inform them of the news formally.

These soldiers had been acting on autopilot because they weren't aware that their circumstances had changed and so their behaviour needed to change accordingly. We too often act as we always have done, because we don't stop to reassess our circumstances and realize that there is a better way of being. Just like the Japanese garrisons, we don't always have radio contact with reality!

Challenge

PART THREE

Take the statements you rewrote in Part Two of this challenge (see pages 128) and decide how you want to replace this reaction by something that will make your life easier and more pleasant! Here are some examples, but it's important for you to take the time to make up your own too:

- I choose to let queues frustrate me but next time I'm in one I will strike up a conversation with someone to pass the time.

- I decide to get annoyed by rude people but in future I will laugh at what they do or say and be grateful that I'm not them!

- I allow criticism to depress me but from now on I'll see what I can learn from it and if it's not justified, I'll ignore it.

- If you want to change how you feel or what you do, this is a key exercise to do.

Affirmation

The only things that stand in my way are my thoughts. As I change my thoughts to positive and encouraging ones, I change my life.

The next step is to practise your new behaviour. If you put the same amount of energy and determination that you have been wasting on unwanted habits into empowering new behaviour, you will see changes very quickly.

Like a child discovering for the first time that the touch of a button can make a light go on or off, so we sometimes need to flick a switch repeatedly to be convinced it works. Many ex-smokers will still refer to themselves as smokers and say that they could give in to the lure of cigarettes at any time. Over time, they usually see that practice turns them into non-smokers, or rather, people who choose not to smoke. The change happens in the brain in an instant, but we usually need confirmation over time that it's worked.

Often, we take the power of our minds for granted. A lot of people are more interested in learning how to operate their mobile phones than learning how to operate and use their minds more effectively. If you're serious about making your life better, the way you rewire your mind and the thoughts you allow yourself to dwell on, are of the utmost importance.

You already have some positive connections wired into your brain, but as you continue to DIY your life there may be times when you discover something else that needs a little rewiring. It may be that you need a whole new connection or maybe you just need to use a dimmer switch on your emotions. Remember to return to the exercises in this step whenever you want to establish a new habit.

One to Watch

GROUNDHOG DAY

Watch this film for some inspiration about breaking patterns of behaviour and rewiring your brain.

Chapter 7
Decluttering

Many people have clutter in their homes. And just as the cupboard under the stairs accumulates rubbish over time, so our minds get clogged up with worries and day-to-day trivia. When we've had enough of the stuff in our homes, we donate it to charity, sell it at a car boot sale, offer it to friends or chuck it in the bin. What can we do with behaviour we no longer want? Can we cleanse ourselves of old resentments? Where can we put the worries that we can do nothing about? We're hardly going to give them away!

First of all we need to be sure that we're ready to let go of all our stuff.

Snapshot

There is an old episode of a well-known sitcom where the housemates are getting rid of their old sofa. It's worn down, the cushions have lost all their spring and padding and it's dusty and fusty. But as it comes time to say goodbye to the sofa, one of the housemates throws himself on it with great drama and says a sentimental goodbye, worthy of an old and dear friend. He's genuinely hurting that the sofa has to go!

Often, even when we know that it's time to chuck things out, we'll cling on to them because we've grown attached to them. This is not only true of possessions but also of emotions. We hold them because they've been around for so long. This attachment is usually irrational because we may know they're not doing us any good and we may not even enjoy having them. We often talk of comfort zones but the ironic thing is that these zones are usually very uncomfortable if not downright painful.

Snapshot

Greg stares at his desk as he listens to an irate customer on the phone. He notices the tightness in his shoulders as he looks at the unanswered urgent memos, the to do list's, the unread business pages, the half drunk cup of super strength coffee and a ton of other office paraphernalia. His heart rate quickens as the red light flashes on his phone to indicate another call waiting, his secretary is wildly waving her arms about to tell him he should be in a meeting, and to top it all off "You have mail!" pops up on his screen. It's probably his girlfriend reminding him of their half-finished argument over their half-organised wedding. He's desperate for the loo but hasn't had time to leave his desk and his stomach is clenched in protest that lunch should have been hours ago. His head is throbbing with outstanding this and unsolved that, his fist clenches as he remembers the home team lost last night, his secretary is losing

---

> control and he's about to wet himself. He doesn't know which way to turn and feels rage rising inside his body. If only he could find his damn stress ball!

Tense, nervous headache? Probably just from reading this. A standard day in the office for some people and my idea of hell on earth. When ever I read this I find myself screwing up my face, hunching my shoulders, clenching my jaw and feeling totally ill at ease in my stomach. Just thinking about mental clutter and stress makes me feel as bad as Greg! But Greg is so used to holding on to his clutter that it seems completely normal to him.

You too may think that the way you're feeling is normal. But once an old habit has been ousted and a new one adopted, we often realize that what we used to hold onto was outdated and actually in our way.

Client case study

A client of mine, Adam, used to get very jealous when his girl friend, Kate would talk to other men. She was very pretty and bubbly and attracted a lot of attention and Adam couldn't help but worry that she would find more interesting or attractive men to be with. One day, after he'd stormed out of a party in green-eyed rage, he confronted her and accused her of flirting unnecessarily. Kate was totally shocked that her behaviour had induced such a response and pointed out that Adam also attracted attention wherever he went and that she found it flattering rather than threatening.

Adam came to see me with this story and I helped him to become reassured by Kate's response. He decided that he would change his behaviour, rather than risk losing her and began to see the admiration she got as a reflection of his good taste and own attractiveness.

Whilst it took some practice, conscious effort and a few initial hiccups, Adam realised how much more relaxed and even happier he felt by looking at it in this way. In addition, his relationship with Kate became stronger as he felt more comfortable with himself.

Picture a sponge when it's sodden with water; it feels heavy and is hard to use because it's so saturated. Imagine clenching your fist and squeezing out all that water, feeling the lightness and buoyancy of the empty sponge in your hand and the potential it has to be filled up again. We have so many habits soaked up in our brains that we are often sodden with them, and they've been there so long that they feel stagnant and stale. We need to squeeze them out, feel light again and then use the room to absorb new ways of behaving and looking at things. Sometimes this means admitting that our clutter is not doing us any good.

> **To err is human; to admit it, superhuman.**
>
> Doug Larson

Challenge

BECOME A MARTIAN

This is the year, or maybe it's next year, when scientists hope to finally discover whether or not there is life on Mars and I'm sure many of them have dreamed about what is up there. Let's say that Martians do exist and that they are planning an expedition to Earth, but they really want to know what goes on inside the human mind and body. And let's also pretend that you are a Martian who gets beamed down into your own body. You are to observe and examine what goes on there and then change it for the better.

As part of this mission, you have access to all your memories and knowledge. You know your emotional history and all your fears, passions, strengths and weaknesses. You see everything through your eyes, but you're not critical or judgemental, you just see what happens and how you let it affect you. Once you're inside your body, you're in total control: you have the power to change the way you think and react to things and therefore to transform your life, both physically and emotionally. The possibilities are endless because you have no concept of limitations or barriers. You are to report your findings in a diary format. This is different from the Life DIY notebook you already have, although I suggest you keep this diary in your book for easy reference. For this exercise to be most effective, you will need to carry your diary around with you so you write down things as they take place, rather than after the event.

This exercise encourages you to be more observant about your life and the array of emotions you experience on a daily basis, seeing it all from a fresh and detached viewpoint. Too many people think that they have no control over how they feel or react, but I hope you're starting to realize quite how much control you do have.

Fill in your diary for at least one full week to ensure you get a decent picture of your life. Observe the different moods you experience and the source of each mood. This diary will illustrate how often your emotions shift and how you're affected by outside stimuli. Here is an example from a client I recently worked with.

Time	Trigger	State
6.30am	Alarm rang	Anxious
7.45am	Stuck in traffic	Stressed and angry

Time	Trigger	State
9.15am	Chatting to a colleague	Laughing and care free
10.30am	Rude to a client	Guilty and stressed
2.00pm	Missed lunch	Tired and impatient
3.15pm	Gave presentations	Nervous and self conscious
4.00pm	Presentation over	Self-critical; starving
6.15pm	Drove past gym	Felt guilty
6.30pm	Got home – saw partner	Short-tempered
7.30pm	Glass of wine and dinner	Began to unwind

Remember that this exercise is all about information gathering, not about judging right or wrong. You must be aware of your actions first, before you can do anything about them. This is only useful, though, if you follow through with your own analysis. At the end of each day, ask yourself these questions:

- What do I notice about this person's behaviour?

- How many of the responses would I want to eliminate to make their life better?

- What options are open to this person at each stage?

It may also help to look back over your notes after a couple of days, when you're sufficiently distanced from them.

You cannot teach a man anything; you can only help him find it within himself.

Galileo

BECOMING YOUR OWN LIFE DIY COACH

You may have heard of life coaches or you may know someone who's worked with one. Often the best way to use an external coach is as, kick-start to change your life, but I believe that everyone should become their own coach in the long term: It's more empowering, realistic and cost-effective.

One of the prerequisites of becoming your own coach is building a better relationship with yourself. In turn, this will help to make your life simpler and easier. What do you think the quality of your life is determined by? I believe it's simple. It comes down to the way we communicate with ourselves.

Maybe you've heard the expression 'Talking to yourself is the first sign of madness', but if that is the case, then we're all mad! We all talk to ourselves through what we call our internal dialogue, a voice in OUR head that commentates on our life. Unfortunately, the majority of people I've worked with don't talk to themselves in a nice way; they run themselves down and give themselves a hard time. If I were to step inside your body and mind for a day, what sort of a day would I have? Would I go to bed thinking, 'What a great day!' or would I think, 'God, that was hard work - all that worry, stress and anxiety"

It may seem sometimes that you have no control over your inner voice but I'll let you into a secret: you have complete and utter control over what it says to you - after all, it is you!

> **The demons' voices grew from whispers to clear convincing ideas. Then I would shake them away. I can do this.**
>
> Bob Beamer

This internal dialogue (also known, amongst other things, as 'self talk' or 'intra-personal dialogue') has become a hot topic of research in recent years. One of the many psycho-physiological studies (Braiker, 1989) suggests that the best approach is to maintain a positive outlook while being realistic. A positive mental attitude does not require self-delusion. Logical and accurate self-talk recognizes areas for improvement and also suggests plans of action and correction. Remember the saying 'If you can't say something good, don't say anything at all'? Well, take this into consideration whilst you communicate with yourself and bear in mind that a helpful way to improve your internal dialogue is to use the affirmations in this book.

To make self-talk more positive and nourishing we must change what goes into our minds - literally, our food for thought. So much of what we let into our heads is the mental equivalent of junk food: it provides little nourishment or sustenance and just fills us up, so there's no room for goodness and energy-giving fuel. But in order to make these changes, we need to recognize these inner messages.

To help you to do this, let's look at the responsibilities of your life DIY coach. These are:

1. To be positive

2. To be encouraging and to stamp out worries or concerns

3. To be gentle and kind to you - not criticizing you, judging you or giving you a hard time

4. To keep you focused on what you want

5. To keep you on track with the rest of the Life DIY process

6. To always put things back into perspective with reassuring words

7. To deal with setbacks and lapses in a constructive and forward-thinking manner

8. To get you to relax by reminding you to breathe deeply and slowly

9.   To help you by suggesting alternative thoughts that make you feel good

10. To remind you to celebrate every day that you are getting stronger and closer to a more fulfilling life

What sort of voice do you want your coach to have? It could be a really upbeat voice that keeps you inspired and positive, it could be soft and gentle, keeping you calm and relaxed, or perhaps it could be seductive and sexy. Or it could be a combination of all of these.

Quick Fix

Say the following statement in your head three times: 'I feel great.' The first time use an upbeat voice, the second time an angry impatient tone and finally try seductive and sexy!

Notice how different you feel according to the way you speak to yourself. Experiment until you find the most encouraging voice for you.

Success is a state of mind. If you want success, start thinking of yourself as a success.

Dr Joyce Brothers

Your Life DIY diary will also help you to become your own coach, as it will increase your awareness of how you feel and how you react to situations.

Another thing that will help you is to imagine that your thoughts are tangible: you can see them, get hold of them and get rid of them if you want to.

A CONVEYOR BELT OF THOUGHTS

You can probably tell I was a fan of The Generation Game! The highlight of the show for me was the game where the contestant would sit in front of various prizes passing by on a conveyor belt: hi-fi, TV, food processor, coffee percolator, garden chairs, cuddly toy, sewing machine and suchlike. At the end of the minute, the contestant got to take home the ones they could remember. There were always some things they really wanted and some things that were thrown in as comedy red herrings - like the cuddly toy. Funnily enough, the contestant would often remember the things they didn't want and completely lose sight of the star prizes. We do the same thing with our thoughts. A lot of the time we know what we should be focusing on but we find that it's the dispiriting and draining thoughts that fill our heads. Way too often I see people stuck with the same old stuff circulating in their minds day after day; it's so habitual that they fail to realize the power they have to break the cycle.

If you don't remember The Generation Game, then maybe you've eaten in a Japanese sushi bar that has a conveyor belt of delicious dishes that travel past you at your table. You get to see it all before you decide, then you help yourself to what you want. I've often sat there and not been quick enough to pick my favourites, but I know that they will come round again a couple of minutes later.

I've also chosen dishes that on closer inspection didn't seem to be quite what I wanted and I've had the chance to put them back.

Too often we view our thoughts in the same way as menu selections: once your food's arrived it's too late to send it back. And quite often someone else's looks more appealing than yours. Well, you'll be pleased to know that you can always send your thoughts back to where they came from and select something better.

Challenge

Imagine you can see your thoughts passing by on a conveyor belt. Start to be choosy about what you pick up. Consider whether it will nourish you or not.

If you pick up something that you don't want, then just put it back and don't worry – if you change your mind it will come round again!

Convincer

What do you think affects the way you feel?. How you feel has an impact on the rest of your life. Everything begins with a thought.

MAKING ROOM

By clearing out rubbish, you will make way for more empowering things in your life. You will have the chance to ensure that you let in encouraging and energizing thoughts and behaviour. Even though we've talked about how a lot of your ideas and beliefs come from other people, you choose what you ignore. And if you make a false start, you can always clear everything away and start again. See each moment as a fresh start. You can always clear everything away and start again. See each moment as fresh and new and a chance to make a difference.

Affirmation

The past is over – long live the present moment.

Quick Fix

From working through this chapter you will
have started to gather together behaviour or
thoughts that you want to change. Pick five
things now that you are going to start thinking
or doing differently with immediate effect.
Write them in your notebook so you can read
them regularly and even put them on a post-
it note somewhere where you will see them
often. This repetition will make it easier for
these thoughts and actions to become new
habits.

1. ....

2. ....

3. ....

4. ....

5. ....

One to Watch

FIELD OF DREAMS

Watch this film for inspiration about following
your dreams, however bizarre they might be!

Chapter 8
Fixing Your Energy Leaks

Let me start this chapter by telling you how your emotions affect your body. Many studies have been done on the effect of negativity on our health. Sadness and depression can lead to the suppression of the immune system (O'Leary, 1990), while poor management of anger has been shown to have a link to heart disease (Fredrickson, Maynard, et al., 1999) and some forms of cancer (Eysenck, 1994).

Barbara Fredrickson at the University of Michigan undertook a study (1998) to prove that cultivating positive emotions was useful in the prevention and treatment of problems arising from negative emotions. The result was her 'broaden-and-build model'. According to this model, negative emotions narrow our ability to think and act, whereas positive emotions broaden the thought-action function that can lead to the development of useful personal resources and positive feelings, that help us to cope with what life throws at us.

Let's look at one particular emotion - fear and what happens in your body when you experience it. Fear is an emotional and physical response to a real or perceived danger and most of us find it powerful and uncomfortable. It puts us on alert, mentally and physically. Brain chemicals called neuro-transmitters are released to give us heightened mental focus. We feel tense, nervous and on edge.

Our fight or flight response system, which prepares our body for action, then kicks in and releases our first hit of adrenaline, a natural hormone. Our muscles tense, our heart rate soars and our breathing rate increases to seize more oxygen. If necessary, chemicals are released to boost physical strength. Blood is directed away from less critical parts of the body and we get tunnel vision and lose a high amount of our hearing. Another big hit of adrenaline is then dumped into our system, heightening these effects and blocking pain. Finally, after the event, the adrenal glands continue to release small amounts of adrenaline, allowing our bodies to readjust after the stressful onslaught.

This process is very useful for some people, like high-performance athletes or those who take part in extreme sports, who make use of it to achieve excellence. But for many of us, this response doesn't help us deal with our fears, like fear of rejection, failure, loss or fear of change, and if prolonged over time, it leads to mental and physical exhaustion.

I've just used fear as an example, but when we experience any negative emotion, there is a similar effect on our physiology. For every action there is a reaction and our body is left to cope with the aftermath.

Conversely, positive emotions have beneficial effects on our health. A study undertaken by Alice Isen demonstrated that positive emotions produce a more flexible, creative and receptive mindset. In addition, other studies (Fridja, 1986) have proved that joyfulness increases the urge to play, explore and invent.

Convincer

Apparently one minute of laughter has the same beneficial effect as 10 minutes of exercise on a rowing machine. Both actions produce endorphins that give us a 'happy rush'.

In some cities in India, there are morning laughter gatherings. On their way to work people stop for half an hour of induced laughter to lift their mood and enhance their physical well-being. They set themselves up for the day with a boost of endorphins and serotonin - the body's natural feel-good drugs.

As you are now aware, we choose to experience different emotions. As different emotions trigger different chemical reactions in our body, in effect, we are our own chemists. What chemical concoctions have you been mixing?

THE ENERGY BALANCE

Imagine being able to look inside a human body that's in good working order. If we were to take a close look we would see the veins, arteries, organs, muscle, bone and fat and could follow the tangible energy flowing around our body. Imagine the blood flowing freely around an intricate network of vessels, carrying oxygen and food to all our cells and taking away the waste and toxins. Imagine the water feeding thirsty tissue and keeping our body in balance and harmony.

If we cut ourselves deeply enough we can see the life force leaking from our bodies. Anyone who has given blood knows how you can feel weak and a bit woozy from this loss. In a similar way, when we are dehydrated or starved of food we can feel weak, tired and irritable. We can replenish these losses fairly quickly. But we are just as likely to experience unseen energy losses.

Dripping water from a tap often goes unnoticed, but over time it all adds up. Sometimes we're not aware of our energy seeping away until we're running on empty.

Snapshot

Harriet was a rock: she was the comforting voice at the end of the phone or the open arms in a time of crisis. She had so much to give to everyone - her children, husband, friends, relatives and even strangers. She gave advice, laughter, love, sustenance and money. She believed that by giving to others, she was proving her worth and justifying her existence.

One day, Harriet couldn't get out of bed. She wasn't able to muster the strength to lift herself from under the covers to go about her day. She slept and slept and slept. After two days, her husband urged her to call the doctor and eventually she gave in.

Harriet was exhausted. She had finally run herself into the ground and was literally drained of all her strength.

Physically she was powerless and mentally she was devoid of all vigour and verve. It took her four weeks to recover to a point where she could go back to work and her life with some element of normality.

What Harriet did to prevent this happening again was to start to put herself first and to use the support of those closest to her.

I, too, learned the hard way what it's like to bleed yourself dry of all your strength by giving too much. I know how it feels to be so exhausted that your head and body are numb; to feel leaden right through to your bones. You literally go into shutdown mode whilst your body takes a hard-earned rest - one that's long overdue.

I don't know the key to success, but the key to failure is to try to please everyone.

Bill Cosby

YOU ARE A RECHARGEABLE BATTERY

Western medicine sees our energy as flowing through the tangible organs in our body: our heart, lungs, blood, stomach, kidneys, liver, muscles, brain and so on. Eastern medicine views energy as an intangible force that flows along meridians. The Chinese call this chi. The Indian principles of Ayurveda state that energy flows through centres called chakras. All these schools of thought agree, however, that when we are in a positive state, our energy is high and when we experience stress or low moods, our energy dips. When we experience positive emotions the body works even more efficiently, but when we have negative feelings or responses, our body still does its usual jobs but also struggles to cope with being knocked off balance.

There are obvious things that recharge energy, like nutritious food, water, sleep, exercise and fresh air. However, in recent years research has shown that our energy is also affected by the way we feel. Think about how exhausted you are after a period of great stress, after worrying and after a long, hard cry. On the other hand, think how good you feel after laughing uncontrollably, being hugged or receiving a piece of uplifting news.

We are like rechargeable batteries. Unlike regular batteries that can only be used once, we can refuel our energy stores when we're run down and can keep on going like the Duracell bunny.

Quick Fix

Tick those items that drain your energy and run down your battery, adding your own to the list if you wish:

☐ Anger   ☐ Anxiety

☐ Blame   ☐ Criticism

☐ Conflict   ☐ Depression

☐ Fear   ☐ Guilt

☐ Inactivity   ☐ Jealousy

☐ Lack of sleep   ☐ Over-activity

☐ Pessimism   ☐ Poor nutrition

☐ Overeating   ☐ Procrastination

☐ Resentment   ☐ Sadness

☐ Self-doubt   ☐ Stress

☐ Worry   ☐ Tension

☐ Alcohol   ☐ Substance abuse

Now tick the items you find particularly energizing, and add your own too:

☐ Drinking water   ☐ Exercise

☐ Friends   ☐ Fresh air

☐ Fun   ☐ Good food

☐ Hugs and kisses   ☐ Kindness

☐ Laughter   ☐ Love

☐ Relaxation   ☐ Optimism

☐ Praise   ☐ Challenges

☐ Regular sleep   ☐ Purpose

☐ Smiling   ☐ Time alone

These nurturing things can recharge our batteries the most when we are present to them. What do I mean by this? Well, I will talk later about the skill of being totally present, but in short it is the ability to be absorbed in what you're doing to the exclusion of everything else.

How many times have you been somewhere or done something amazing, only to have missed out on the full experience, because your thoughts were elsewhere? Sarah was at the theatre the other day and found herself missing half of a crucial scene because she was going back over an argument she'd had earlier on in the day. What a waste of a trip to the theatre!

How many great moments have you let pass you by because your mind was fixated on something else? Don't just be present in your body, be present with your whole self to get the most pleasure and energy from what you do.

Quick Fix

Take a minute to do a quick energy check on your body. Close your eyes and notice how you feel. Do you feel a buzz of energy in your body or a calm flow? Do certain parts of you feel more energised than others? Do you notice any dull or heavy areas? Can you literally feel energy seeping out of you? Or do you have a self-contained circuit of power surging round and round?

What have you done to cause these feelings in your body?

HOW FULL IS YOUR GLASS?

You may have heard people describe themselves as either a person who sees a glass as half full, or one who sees, it as half empty. I expect you all by the end of the workbook to have the 'glass half full' attitude. That will take care of itself, but what I'm more concerned with now, is how full your own glass is.

Client case study

Marie came to see me because she was feeling run down and wasn't sure what was wrong with her life. She looked sapped and sat slumped in the chair. It was obvious that she wasn't giving herself enough mental or physical nourishment.

I took her into my kitchen and handed her two glasses one full of water and one empty one. I told her to imagine that she was the full glass and that the water was her energy stores.

I asked to list all the things in life that took up her energy and as she reeled them off - worry, low self-esteem, blame and so on - I got her to decant the water from one glass to the other. She'd soon run out of water.

'OK,' I said, 'now it's time to see how you put that energy back.'

I asked her to pour the water back into the original glass as she thought of the things that fuelled her. She mentioned a few things but couldn't manage to fill up the glass.

Now it's your turn!

Challenge

Take two glasses - one full of water and one empty one. Think about where your energy goes, and as you do so, decant the water from the full glass to the empty one.

Now think about pouring the energy back into yourself.

What do you do to fill yourself back up? As think about each thing, pour some of the water back into the other glass.

What do you notice by doing this? Is there a balance between outgoing and incoming energy? What drains you the most? What do you need more of?

What some of you may notice is that lots of things you do, people you spend time with or feelings you have, take energy away from you. Some of you may find that you struggled to fill the glass even halfway.

TOO MUCH OF A GOOD THING

There is a common misconception that things you enjoy are not at all draining and therefore if you love your job and enjoy a good social life and significant relationships, it's not possible to get sapped. Sadly, this isn't true for many people. Even the things we relish have their downsides -

especially if we do too much of them. There are elements of most of our lives that take their toll on us and it's the parasitic ones that feed off us quietly that are the ones we really need to learn to deal with or eliminate completely.

I want you to start thinking about your energy as a utility that must be accounted for. Just as we have to pay the bills or feed the meter to keep ourselves in light, heat and modern conveniences, so we need to nourish our souls to keep ourselves thriving rather than just surviving.

To preserve and increase your energy levels, you have to make better choices about what you're going to spend your energy on. You may have to give up a lifelong habit of doing things for other people because you think it makes you a worthwhile human being. If you're a parent, you've probably given a lot of yourself and maybe even at times to the detriment of your own health and happiness One thing I always ask parents is 'What do you want your children to have?' Ultimately they usually want their children to be able to take care of themselves and to feel good about who they are. The best way for a parent to do this, is to feel good about who they are and show their children how it's done.

It may be second nature to live your life with your cup constantly half empty, but I assure you that your first duty as your own life coach is to nourish yourself. It is only when your cup is overflowing that you are really in a position to give anything away.

Affirmation

I deserve the best.

THE BLACK HOLES OF ENERGY

Some of the most common drains of our energy
are anger, fear, guilt, jealousy and worry. Take
guilt, for example. I have first-hand experience of
what it's like to feel guilty about everything! My
mother always thought of others first and I grew
up thinking that this was the correct way to be.
Taking it all too far, I would feel guilty for things
I had or hadn't done and things I couldn't do
anything about. I had a big black hole of guilt that
devoured my energy. What a waste!

Quick Fix

Next time you fall into any of the mental
comfort zones, make this choice:

Either feel that emotion as much as you can –
really allowing it to take you over.

Or just don't bother wasting energy on it at all
and do something else!

I believe that most of the mental comfort zones
we create for ourselves are totally pointless
and should be thrown out altogether, but it is
very unlikely that we will go through life without
accumulating any of them ever again. So what

would be really useful, would be to learn to be accountable for them and their consequences.

STAND UP AND BE ACCOUNTABLE

If you're accountable, you decide to do something about how you feel. Accountability is much more action-oriented than any of the debilitating and draining negative mood states. Take two different examples.

Snapshot

Emma and Richard had started a relationship. It was a casual kind of affair, mainly because Richard dictated when they saw each other and, because she liked him so much, Emma was prepared to fit in around him. One Saturday evening they were at a club having a few drinks and a bit of a dance when Richard disappeared for about an hour, leaving Emma bemused and unamused. He returned with no explanation and they went home. After half an hour of chilled silence, Emma asked Richard where he'd been and why he'd left her for so long on her own. 'There's nothing between us, Emma,' he said. 'I don't feel anything for you, so you'd better go home.' Shocked and baffled, Emma left and Richard felt guilty.

Let's rewind and see what had really happened in the club. Richard had bumped into an ex-girlfriend who had dumped him a couple of years before. They had chatted and whilst there was no chance of them getting back together, it made Richard compare the passion and closeness he had had with his ex to the relaxed and casual nature of his relationship with Emma. His initial reaction was to think that there was nothing substantial between him and Emma and that he should tell her as soon as he could. He felt guilty for seemingly stringing her along and thought that he should now do the right thing. Of course, because he only told Emma half the story, he then felt even guiltier for sending her away without a decent explanation.

Whilst it may not seem logical to everyone, Richard did have a positive intention, but by not explaining his actions he felt like a cad and Emma felt insecure. If he'd been accountable and told Emma how he felt, both of them would have felt better.

Snapshot

William came to me because he had a glut of anger. He continually went out of his way to help his boss, who he knew was under huge amounts of pressure, and he was pressurizing himself in the process. He would regularly stay late and would take work home most weekends, yet his efforts seemed to go unnoticed or, at least, he wasn't given any recognition for them. He was so livid that he had started to experience high blood pressure and was rapidly gaining weight.

I asked William how he could become accountable for his own anger and what effect this would have on his situation. Once he became accountable for the way he felt, what options would be open to him to make his working life better?

William realised that he chose to go the extra mile at work - it had never been asked of him. He also needed to look at why he was doing it: if he was expecting external confirmation of his worth, then he'd be waiting for a long time! He had to become responsible for recognizing his own worth and so started to divert some energy away from work and towards achieving this. He started to fill his cup back up.

WHAT'S IN YOUR BLACK HOLE?

The ancient Greek myth of Sisyphus tells of a man who spent his life pushing a stone ball up a hill. Each time he reached the top, the weight of the ball would overcome him and it would roll back down the hill.

You can roll your burden around with you all you like, but if it hasn't done you any good so far, what are the chances of it doing you any good in the future? Every time you reach the top of your mountain and are about to get a different view on things, that heavy old ball will just drag you back down.

Challenge

In America, there are signs on the freeways telling you to STOP and go back if you're driving on the wrong side of the road. Start to use your own STOP sign to help you stop experiencing emotions you don't want.

Picture a STOP sign in front of you. Make it big, bright and bold.

Now, loudly and clearly, say the word 'Stop' inside your head.

Now simultaneously see the sign and hear that command to STOP over and over again.

Repeat this 10-15 times until you're used to seeing the sign and hearing the signal.

The next time you begin to feel an emotion you don't want, like guilt or fear, immediately recall the STOP sign to prevent yourself going down that same old road.

When you have more awareness about what drains you, you can make choices about how to balance yourself. Over time, demands on your energy can change, and as they do, it's important to maintain your energy stores and to stop any leaks.

Any time you want to check yourself, do a quick body scan of how you feel, just as you did earlier (see page 164). What I want you to have is a free-flowing circuit of energy that feels effortless.

One to Watch

AMELIE

Watch Amelie to see the joy that can be experienced by doing things just for the fun of them!

Chapter 9
The Emotional Extractor Fan

Have you ever seen how long you can hold your breath for? You take in a big gasp of air and then you wait and wait and wait. You begin to feel a bit woozy and odd and then your throat starts to constrict; you try to take in more air through your nose and then hold and hold and hold until you can't take it any more. You sink down with the expulsion of air and the relief of relaxation, and then wonder what possessed you to do it! It's like needing to cry and trying really hard to hold back the tears, or bursting for the loo and not able to go - there is no relief like the one when you finally let go!

Quick Fix

Take a moment to tighten yourself up as much as you can.

Start with your feet and grip your toes, tense your leg muscles, constrict your abdomen, clench your fists and arm muscles, screw up your face and hold your breath.

Feel the effect all over your body. Hold this for a few seconds and then just let everything go. Really breathe out and feel the liberation and calm that come over you.

It's common for us to think we're relaxed when we're not because we're so used to holding ourselves in a state of semi tension. We think it's normal and it's only when we get exhausted or have a migraine that we realize something is wrong. You may have heard people say that disease is caused by dis-ease and if you've ever been very stressed or upset, you will know what it's like to feel the very real physical effect that these feelings have on your body.

Holding on to anger is like grasping a hot coal with the intent of throwing it at someone else: you are the one who gets burned.

Buddha

Client case study

Annabel came to see me because she was experiencing regular headaches, breakouts of spots and stomach upsets and was getting very little sleep. She kept saying to herself that she shouldn't feel tense or upset - after all, she had everything: a well-paid job, a boyfriend (when lots of her friends were unhappily single), her own flat, and a supportive and close family. She had no reason to be unhappy or unfulfilled. She felt she had to pull herself together and couldn't understand why she felt so low and drained.

On talking to Annabel more I learned that she had an excessive workload, a threat of redundancy, a less than nourishing relationship and an ageing mother to whom she gave a lot of attention. She was under a considerable amount of stress and she just didn't realize it. Whenever this realization neared the surface, she would push it back under because life had to go on. She had been brought up with the age-old adages 'Don't worry, be happy!' and 'Count your blessings!' and wanting more seemed almost greedy.

I pointed out to Annabel that by stifling her emotions and 'just getting on with things' they had grown to the point of bursting to the surface in the form of physical ailments. It was her body saying to her, 'Wake up and smell the coffee, honey! You need to do something about your life! And until you do, I'll continue to niggle you.'

'It would have been better if Annabel had allowed herself to be worried about her job or concerned for her mother's health and then moved on to doing something about them. If she'd done this, she probably wouldn't have suffered as she did from denying and resisting her concerns.

We are resilient to a point, but if we push ourselves too far, the signs of strain will show up somewhere. It's like holding your thumb over a leaking pipe; eventually the pressure becomes too much. We all need to release our emotions. Wouldn't it be great to have a flush you could use when you wanted to cleanse yourself of a yucky feeling?

Our bodies are designed to expel what we don't want - that's why we have waste mechanisms. We exhale toxins and excess gases and we sweat through our pores. Our bodies naturally want to express our feelings too, but we are often conditioned not to show them - 'stiff upper lip and all that'.

TAKE A DEEP BREATH

I'm sure you've all heard the advice 'Take a deep breath and count to 10': it's usually doled out when someone feels stressed, angry or overwhelmed and it's been said so often that it's often not given the credit that it deserves.

There is a saying that the simplest things in life are the most effective and breathing is a prime example of this. The way you breathe affects the way you feel and by making some simple adjustments to your breathing, you can influence the way you deal with emotions and therefore improve your physical well-being.

Quick Fix

Get a watch or clock that measures seconds and sit somewhere comfortable.

Focus on your breathing, as you breathe in through your nose and out through your nose or mouth.

Count how many breaths you take in one minute, breathing as you normally do.

Rest for a minute and then repeat the exercise but this time making a conscious effort to deepen your breaths, really filling your lungs.

Notice how good it feels to breathe in this way.

Try to carry it on throughout the day.

Men breathe on average 12-14 times per minute and women breathe 15-17 times per minute. Quicker breathing is often termed 'emergency breathing': the body is stressed and in a state of alert. In my experience, people who breathe more than the average. Are often highly stressed because they are sending signals to their body that there is an imminent emergency and so the body prepares for fight or flight.

Quick breathing also tends to be shallow and shallow breathing has very real detrimental effects on our physical health. Our blood transports oxygen to every cell in the body and takes away toxins; in fact 70 per cent of the body's toxins are expelled through our breath. Less than a tenth of a litre of blood flows through the top of our lungs every minute, compared to two thirds of a litre through the middle. But down at the bottom of our lungs, well over a litre of blood flows through each minute. When we breathe deeply we send fresh supplies of oxygen down into the pit of our lungs, thus feeding our body more generously with the air it needs.

Challenge

Lie down comfortably and place a book on your stomach, just over your belly button.

As you breathe, notice the rise and fall of your chest and stomach and focus on making the book rise.

As you breathe out, simply say to yourself, 'Relax.' Continue for a few minutes.

Practise this at least once a day and during the rest of the day, think about filling up the whole of your lungs with air.

When you're extracting emotions you don't want, as well as ousting them from your mind, you want to expel them physically from your body. So I want you to become more observant of your breathing patterns and how they change according to your moods. See if you can control the way you feel through the way you breathe.

WATCH YOUR LANGUAGE

Watch your language, too, because even what you say can affect your breathing. What do you think happens if you say to yourself, 'I'm so stressed' or 'I'm frightened' or 'I can't cope'? Well, the primitive part of your brain responds to what it perceives to be a dangerous situation and adapts your breathing to cope. Send relaxing messages to that part of your brain instead and see what happens when you work on your breathing from multiple angles.

> **Snapshot**
>
> Two monks were walking together when they
> came to a stretch of water. Standing nearby
> was a beautiful woman who asked them for
> help to get across. The elder monk carried her
> over the water and then resumed his walk with
> the younger monk.
>
> After a few minutes of tense silence, the
> younger monk said, 'We are not allowed to
> look at, let alone touch, women.'
>
> The elder monk replied, 'I put her down on the
> other side of the water; you are still carrying
> her.'

MOVE ON!

Remember baby Bobby burning his hand on
the oven and releasing his pain by crying? After
that his body was back to a state of balance.
Children often go through a number of feelings
in a short space of time: they smile, frown, bawl,
kick, scream, laugh and then smile again and
usually fall asleep from the intensity of it all! Our
early childhood is one of the only times we are
allowed to release our emotions uncensored and
even then some adults try to stifle this natural
instinct and encourage children to maintain their
composure no matter what.

I realize that there are some situations where it's
not appropriate to release your feelings, but we
can all find the right time and space to do so to

avoid the festering and emotional constipation
that otherwise occurs.

I mentioned earlier the characteristics that we've
lost since our early childhood. The gift of being
present is something that very few of us have
retained. Often when we get angry or annoyed or
stressed or worried, we hold on to the emotion for
a long time: hours, days, sometimes even weeks or
months. If you were to add up the amount of time
spent experiencing negative emotions, you might
find that you don't have much time for anything
else. In fact, when clients come to me because
they're dominated by a particular negative
feeling, thought or habit, I always ask them what
they'd do with the extra time they'd gain if they
weren't experiencing that emotion.

> **Time is our most valuable asset, yet we tend to
> waste it, kill it, and spend it rather than invest it.**
>
> Jim Rohn

I remember one client who would always find
something to be anxious about. We worked out
that from the moment he woke up to the moment
he went to sleep, a large proportion of his day was
spent being anxious. I asked him, 'If you weren't
being anxious, what would you do with all the time
that you had available to you?'

I also explained to him the simple truth that if you
always do what you've always done, you'll always
get what you've always got. The secret for him,
and for anyone else who wants to break any
pattern of behaviour, is to replace old thoughts

and emotions with new ones. I don't want to turn you into robots that feel nothing. Experiencing a wide range of emotions makes life interesting. There are times when you want to feel annoyed or sad, and that's OK as long as you become accountable for the way you feel. Allow yourself to feel the emotion and then move on. Children often acknowledge that they have something to be upset about (even if they're too young to label it), but they let it go quickly because there are many more fun things to do than be moody or angry. I'm sure you can think of more fun things that you'd like to do with your time tool.

> **Most people are about as happy as they make up their minds to be.**
>
> Abraham Lincoln

Challenge

In order to replace our unwanted emotions, it's essential to recognize what triggered them. As you're filling in your Life DIY diary, remember to use the information to learn about your responses to situations. You can also look at how long you let things affect you. How could you help yourself by letting go?

Remember, it's OK to have negative feelings and thoughts now and again ~ you're only human, after all. There are also times when it's useful to feel angry or frightened; for example, if a car is about to hit you, you want your fight-or-flight response to kick in so you can run out of danger. But feeling angry at being stuck in a traffic jam or a queue when you can't do anything about it, is only going to make you feel bad.

Challenge

This is a symbolic exercise for you to begin the process of clearing out negative emotions. Pick someone you feel mildly angry towards or a situation that is concerning you. I want you to start with something minor as we will be building up to more significant events through this chapter.

1. Sit somewhere comfortable with your back supported and your feet flat on the ground.

2. Focus your attention on the rise and fall of your chest and stomach as you begin to breathe more deeply.

3. Think of the person/situation and the feeling you have about them/it. Imagine that emotion collecting inside you. Give it a colour or consistency so that it feels very real.

4. As you breathe out, imagine that each breath is filling up a big balloon with this negative emotion. Breathe out with force to expel the emotion.

5. When the balloon is full, let go of it and see it flyaway into the distance until it becomes a speck on the horizon and disappears.

> 6. Repeat this process as many times as you need either for the same person/event or for different ones.

Take a moment to think about your mental and emotional health. There are many things we do, whether we're aware of it or not, to relieve mental and physical tension: exercise, smoke, drink, eat, have sex, take drugs, gamble, play sport, watch sport, drive fast, get violent. Whilst some of these have their value, some (and I'm sure you can see which ones) are destructive. It's also important to recognize what caused the tension in the first place and address the root cause, rather than covering up the problem only to be confronted with it time and time again.

THE 'F' WORD!

I have worked with many people who have carried around a lot of blame, anger and resentment and a desire for revenge. When I have suggested that it might be better for their health and their future for them to forgive, it's often as if I've just said the other 'F' word. People flinch, shudder, cringe and look at me in horror and disgust! Forgiveness is a bitter pill for many people to swallow, but it can be a very powerful choice.

The main reason why people don't want to forgive is because they think that forgiveness means that they condone what happened to them. This pattern is very apparent in people who have suffered abuse, be it mental, emotional or physical. But it's not the way I see forgiveness.

Forgiveness, to me, is about freeing yourself. It's not about the people who've hurt you or taken advantage of you: you can't do anything about them and what goes on in their heads, but you can look after yourself and liberate yourself from the prison of your anger or resentment.

There are huge emotional costs to allowing someone to have power over how you feel (often long after the actual event) and if these feelings could be measured or weighed in some way, I'm sure you'd see just how much of a burden they are. It's like rising damp, it's easy to paint over it and hide it temporarily, but until it's treated properly, it keeps spreading and becoming more pronounced. Effective Life DIY involves getting rid of the things that make your living conditions unhealthy and difficult, not painting over them.

Snapshot

In America, a man sued McDonald's, claiming that they were to blame for his weight issue. He said that the restaurant chain should have made it clear to him that the food they were serving was not healthy (as he had thought it was) and that this negligence on their part led to his obesity and ill health.

If this man is ever to sort out his health issues, he will need to give up blaming McDonald's and become accountable for his situation.

Our culture is becoming increasingly blame-focused, with the popularity of suing people at an all-time high. Now, it's within your rights to sue someone who's negligent and there are definitely times when this is an effective and appropriate response. But for other situations, suing is just a way of assigning responsibility to someone else for our own misfortunes and the circumstances of our decisions.

Owning a problem, and therefore the solution, is key to dealing with it. It comes back to being accountable for the way you feel.

Affirmation

There is no need to blame anyone.

Snapshot

A teacher at school physically abused my brother when he was about 12 years old. He was young and innocent and to be violated in this way was a major injustice and incredibly damaging. The experience emotionally scarred him and he kept it to himself for years.

As is common with people who are abused, he started to convince himself that there was something wrong with him and became very self-conscious. Understandably, many negative emotions like fear, anger and blame built up inside him and started eating him up. The abuse continued long after the event as my brother carried the emotional anguish inside his head. The more he continued to process what had happened, replaying it in his mind, the more he experienced these harmful emotions and the more powerful they became.

The belief that something was wrong with him, coupled with these feelings, led him to begin to abuse himself both mentally and physically. I'm sure that our parents put his behaviour down to being a teenager, but he became more distant and the fun-loving, happy-go-lucky boy we once knew disappeared.

He escaped the mental anguish by 'getting out of it' with drugs. I remember him telling me years later, after he had become a drugs counsellor, that if people don't like what's going on inside their heads, the easiest thing for them to do is to 'get out of their head'. Eventually he was sent to prison for drug dealing and there he found the courage to talk for the first time about being abused. This was the first step in his forgiveness.

His process of healing has been a long one, but one thing is for sure: he is no longer plagued by his experience and he has forgiven the person who harmed him all those years ago. When I say he has forgiven this person, what I mean is he no longer allows this person to have any effect on his life. It's not that he's forgotten what happened, but that the event no longer tarnishes his existence.

More importantly, he has forgiven himself for the way he treated himself for so long. He has replaced the emotions he didn't need with positive emotions like love, happiness and joy, shared with his wife and two children. He is now a therapist and has devoted himself to helping others who've had similar experiences.

We have all been abused on some level. Some of you may find that a difficult concept to take in, but that's only because of the common meaning that abuse has nowadays. What I mean is we've been abused by our conditioning, and many of us have abused ourselves as well.

Challenge

THE PROTECTIVE FORCE FIELD

Only use this exercise once you are sure that you want to forgive the people who've done you wrong. If there are a number of people, start with the ones who've had a smaller influence and be patient and take a break before you move on to the others.

1. Write a list of the people you want to forgive. Choose one person to start with.

2. Sit somewhere quiet and comfortable with your feet firmly planted on the ground and begin to focus on your breathing.

3. Imagine you're sitting inside a big protective bubble or sphere that no one can enter. It acts as a defensive force, protecting you from outside influences. Allow yourself to feel totally safe and secure.

4. Outside your protective sphere, make a picture of the person you wish to forgive.

5. Push the picture into the distance so you can barely make out the image. Make it fuzzy and blurry.

6. Say to yourself or out loud: 'I forgive you, [name], for what you've done and free myself from past hurts.'

7. Repeat this a number of times until the image disappears and/or you feel freed and empowered.

Challenge

A LETTER

Write a letter to each of those people you wish to forgive.

Allow yourself to get your resentments down onto paper, but tell these people that you forgive them. Let them know that you intend to leave them in your past and that you're going to be getting on with your life without their influence.

I advise you not to send the letter but to see
it as a symbolic act of forgiveness, something
that you are doing for yourself. Either throw
the letter away or burn it.

These exercises can be very useful in removing
the negative emotions that take up a lot of our
energy. Once they have gone, there will be plenty
of room for new thoughts to help you on your
quest for happiness and fulfilment.

It's important to recognise that many people
get enormous benefit from talking about their
experiences with a qualified professional. If this
is something that you feel would benefit you or
someone else, see it as a positive step, as it's
healthy to admit that you need help. A good
starting point would be to speak to your GP to get
an appropriate referral.

JUDGEMENT DAY

I have spent many years making judgements
about people and subsequently trying to change
those people, so that they would think in a similar
way to me. I now know that this doesn't work and
that the answer for me is to accept people the
way that they are and perhaps suggest that they
consider a different perspective, if I think it may be
of use to them. The important thing, though, is for
me to consider their point of view first.

For many people, every day is Judgement Day
and a lot of the judgements we make about others
are really reflections of our own insecurities. The

behaviour that you judge most harshly and most frequently is probably an issue that you've yet to resolve in yourself. We often fail to realize that what we say about others actually applies to ourselves. If we did, we'd be more careful about our comments.

A lot of the female clients I've worked with, who want to improve their self-esteem and body confidence, tell similar stories. They will be at a party or in a crowded place and will make continual judgements about other women based on the way they look. These can be positive or negative: 'She's much more attractive than me, so her life must be perfect', 'She shouldn't be wearing that, she's way too fat' or 'She's so slim and beautiful - what a bitch!'

Men also tend to make judgements about other men. They form an opinion of someone according to what they do for a living, how much they earn, where they live, how they live and what they look like.

The outcome is usually the same: the person making these judgements feels even worse, becuase they are reinforcing the negative beliefs they have about themselves.

My aim is to make you a better judge so that you are less critical of yourself and others.

> **When you judge another, you do not define them, you define yourself.**
>
> Wayne Dyer

It's not a question of whether our judgements are true or not, as a lot of the time we never find out. What's important is the impact these judgements have on us.

So I want you to be aware of the judgements you form about others. It's hard to completely stop judging people, but try to pay less attention to your judgements and just observe your thoughts instead. See if you can control the effect your observations have on you.

Quick Fix

The next time you catch yourself making a judgement that produces a negative response, ask yourself: 'What's in this for me?'

Be aware of the side-effects of the judgement you're making and observe something different instead.

One to Watch

PAY IT FORWARD

Just watch it!

Chapter 10
Tightening Your Security System

Why do lots of people have alarms in their homes? They have them to protect themselves and their belongings; some people have them because they're afraid. Do you know that some houses with alarm boxes on the outside don't actually have alarm systems? The boxes are just deterrents for burglars. The houses are seemingly well-protected - how would you know if the system was a false one? You'd probably have to break and enter to find out.

Similarly, the general school of thought is that if your life looks good on the outside, you must feel great on the inside So millions of people look for quick fixes to feel better about themselves: miracle diets, manic exercise regimes, material possessions and plastic surgery. But the cover doesn't always tell you the whole story. I don't believe that there is any correlation between how attractive or wealthy you are and how comfortable you are with yourself. Many a rich, beautiful person doesn't like what they see when they look in the mirror or doesn't feel proud of themselves when they go to bed at night.

How many people do you know who are very secure in themselves, who know and like themselves, who are happy with who they are and what they have? Sadly, insecurity is a growing epidemic in the Western world

When did we start feeling insecure? For many of us it all started when we were children. Young children are very vulnerable and at the same time open to what's going on around them, but because they learn by copying people around them, they pick up many insecurities.

I recently went to my niece's fourth birthday party. I really enjoy being around young children and find their energy and enthusiasm for life fun and infectious. Many children are free from hang-ups, insecurities and other negative emotions. At the party, there was plenty for them to do: food to eat, swings to play on, barnyard animals to learn about and an adventure playground to explore It was amazing to see these little boys and girls just running around doing what they wanted. There was no structure to the party until some of the adults decided that it was time to play games.

The first game was musical chairs. For those of you who don't know the rules of this game, here's a quick lesson: everyone moves to music around a lot of chairs. When the music stops, everyone has to rush to sit on a chair but there aren't enough for everyone, so one person - usually the slowest - gets left out.

Once this game started, the atmosphere totally changed. The first girl who had to sit out began to cry; she really liked the game and was upset about having to sit on the edge and watch her friends having fun. She cried for the entirety of the game. As more children dropped out, it was interesting to watch their reactions. Some were sad, while others just got on with something else.

It seems so strange that children start to interpret things so differently from a young age. Some of the messages that children can pick up from playing games like this are: 'I'm not good enough', 'I'm not as good as everyone else', 'You have to be the best', 'It's wrong to lose' or 'There's something wrong with me.' As we've seen, as children get older they often carry these kind of beliefs with them and when a similar situation arises - perhaps not passing an exam, not getting the person they want or being overlooked for a promotion – they strengthen this belief.

Affirmation

I release all self-doubt and criticism.

Challenge

Write down five things you don't like about yourself.

1. ....

2. ....

3. ....

4. ....

5. ....

They can be physical characteristics, character traits or habits. Now write down five things you do like about yourself, things that you're proud of, that you really appreciate.

....

....

....

....

....

What do you notice about this exercise? Which part did you find easier to do? I'd guess you completed the list of dislikes quicker than the list of likes. We're not brought up to draw attention to our positive points and we spend far too much time comparing ourselves to others, rather than to the best we can be. Then lack of contentment with what we have sets many of us on a long arduous journey of perfection and control.

ARE YOU A CONTROL FREAK?

We live in a society that respects control, whether it's control over what you eat, control over your work or control over your feelings. Have you ever heard the piece of advice 'Don't let them see that they've hurt you'? Heaven forbid we should be perceived as a real flesh-and-blood person who has a heart.

Control is a funny thing: most of us want to be in control of our lives and to a certain extent we need to be to function. But can we be in control and still be free? Does being too controlled mean that you're actually out of control? Anyone who has ever been the victim of their own controlling behaviour will know how frightening it can be to suddenly find yourself freewheeling. What, no calorie counting? What, no hourly hand-washing? What, no familiarity?

Snapshot

Sarah, aged 17, was on holiday with friends. She was at a particularly low point and her male companions found her dieting very hard to relate to. She would allow herself a daily ration of one apple and a jar of baby food: no room to be out of control, no thought needed.

One evening, after a day of carrying her heavy rucksack, her body cried out for food: it had had enough and was sending her big signals. There was a chink in her steely armour and she bought a baked potato. She remembers holding it for a while and feeling sick at the thought of giving in. Shaking, she took a bite ... and dissolved into tears, much to the shock and fear of her friends.

She'd lost control, and she believed she was worthless and weak.

One of the hardest things to do, and one of the most useful, is to not relate to our insecurities and fears. If we're afraid to be who we really are because we don't think that the genuine article is good enough, we often live by a set of rules and restrictions that we believe gives us more worth. But this isn't the answer to long-term security.

THE COMMONEST FEAR

A lot of my work involves helping clients who have fears and phobias and I'm always astounded by the lengths to which people will go when it comes to avoiding their fears: the agoraphobic who didn't leave her house for 25 years; the man who seriously limited what he ate for fear of being sick; the lady who never wore buttons and couldn't even look at them.

People talk about being frozen with fear and the initial response when we're confronted with the unknown is to tighten up to protect ourselves. For example, if we're afraid of being hurt by a loved one, we tighten our hearts; when faced with a concept that runs counter to our beliefs, we restrict our openness and become 'narrow-minded'; if we're giving a presentation and are afraid of making a fool of ourselves, our throats constrict; athletes, nervous in the heat of competition, will often physically tighten up; those who are afraid of needles or pain will screw up their faces and clench their fists, their fear gripping them wholly.

Some of the most common fears in our society are fear of not being good enough, fear of rejection, fear of being alone, fear of looking stupid or of exposing ourselves, fear of being hurt and fear of failure. I look at these issues and they seem to boil down to one thing: the fear that there's something wrong with us. Anxiety about not fitting in and being accepted, greatly affects our behaviour.

I've written a whole workbook on fears and how to overcome them, so I'm aware that I'm distilling this subject greatly here. I also know that even people who are happy with who they are, come across situations that make them feel uncomfortable or inadequate from time to time. I do believe, however, that if we were all comfortable in our skin, almost all our negative emotions would disappear and we would feel more secure.

Quick Fix

Stop saying 'I'm not ... enough:

Think about whether it's realistic for you to improve that aspect of yourself by comparing yourself to the best you think you can be.

If it is, then decide to do something about it.

Affirmation

I let go of all my fears and doubts.

Another key characteristic of our fears is that they tend to become self-fulfilling: fear of failure can keep you stuck in a rut and feeling more like a loser than you did before; fear of rejection means that you often don't try to do something so you still don't feel good enough; fear of being vulnerable can lead to defensive behaviour which means you not only hurt others but also hurt yourself in the process; fear of being alone drives many people to be with the wrong person - which, ironically, makes you feel even more isolated. So why do we have these fears?

THE MASKS WE WEAR

I have a friend who was afraid of being in her house alone when her husband was away. She finally decided to get a dog. Although he took a lot of looking after, he helped her to feel more secure. She got a crutch for herself, but it doesn't mean she got rid of her fear. There are many different crutches to make us feel safer and more secure, in particular possessions, people we can lean on and alcohol and drugs.

Tony Adams, the famous England and Arsenal central defender wrote a very honest autobiography, 'Addicted', detailing his football career and the effect of alcoholism on his life. In his youth he was so into his football training that he didn't drink when all his friends were discovering booze. Then everything changed during the 1987/88 season when he felt as though he had become the 'scapegoat for the ills of the English game'. He was given the nickname 'Donkey Adams' by the fans and faced cries of 'Eeyore' for his blunders on the pitch.

Adams admits that whilst this motivated him in public, in private it hurt like hell and he turned to alcohol to numb the pain. He says, 'I drank because I was frightened and I was frightened because I drank. I couldn't tell which came first.' Alcohol dulled the fear and hid his unwillingness to face up to the emotions he was experiencing.

Being in the public eye can magnify someone's dependence issues and the press loves to blow things out of proportion, but to some degree most people have their own numbing devices to help them suspend reality. Whether it's consuming the contents of your fridge to make you feel better about your loneliness or the £500 shopping spree to deal with a bad day at the work, the problems still exist. Whether it's mindless sex with a stranger to satisfy your craving for intimacy or drugs to boost your confidence, the underlying issues are still there the morning after.

DETACH YOURSELF

You would think that in a time when so many things are plentiful in the West we would have a pretty tight grip on happiness. We have the highest standard of living in the history of mankind, yet few of us seem happy with our lot.

> *The greedy search for money or success will almost always lead men into unhappiness. Why? Because that kind of life makes them depend upon things outside themselves.*
>
> Andre Maurois

We believe that many of our possessions are necessities: mobile phones, televisions, cars, hi-fis, refrigerators and, of course, computers. They are supposed to make our lives easier. But what have they done to many of us?

Many people now believe that these material goods are significant in attaining happiness and fulfilment: the path to the Western dream is paved with white goods, designer clothes and the latest technology.

Now, I'm not saying that in DIYing your life you have to get rid of all these things, though what I'm going to suggest might appear radical and a little hard. I want you to be aware of the attachments you have and what they're doing for you. And I want you to consider detaching yourself from needing anything (beyond the real necessities) or anyone in your life.

The reason behind this is for you to feel complete again. I'm not saying that you need to get out of your relationships or that you have to sell up and move to a desert island. I just want you to realize that the only attachment you need is to yourself.

> *It's good to have money and the things that money can buy, but it's good, too, to make sure you haven't lost the things that money can't buy.*
>
> George Horace Lorimer

THE OTHER HALF

One very popular attachment for people is other people; the very phrase 'my other half' suggests you're only complete when you're with someone else. This may explain why so much effort is put into finding the perfect match. But how can you match perfectly two unique objects? Surely they can only complement each other?

This is not about giving up loving someone or having human connections. It's about not feeling the need to own or be owned and to realize that you are a person in your own right: you are capable of being alone even if you think you're not. You are good enough on your own.

The most fruitful relationships are often ones where two people love each other so much that they allow each other to make their own choices and each has enough self-worth not to be threatened by the other doing things by themselves.

Perhaps one reason why relationships break down is because of the insecurities people have about themselves. When two people get together it's often quite easy to hide their insecurities and then after the honeymoon period, they tend to come to the surface. Then you not only have your own insecurities to deal with, but someone else's too. The more you feel good about yourself, the better position you will be in to have loving and meaningful relationships. When you feel good about who you are, you can allow those around you to be who they are, without you having to control their every move.

The key is not to be selfish or totally selfless, but to be yourself. See if you can relate to others from a position of love and support whilst suspending your own beliefs, values and expectations of them: this is unconditional love.

Isn't it better to put one and one together to get two, rather than needing two halves to make a whole?

LET THE PAST PASS YOU BY

The past has gone. Too many people are still attached to the good old days: the way they used to look or the love they once had. An even higher number are still tied to the flotsam and jetsam that should have long gone: mistakes, difficult times and periods of hurt and anguish. The more we attach ourselves to the past, the less we are able to enjoy the present. All you can do is learn from things you wish you'd done differently and use the things you did well to fuel the present. It's called the present for a reason: because the best gift you can give to yourself is to enjoy each moment as it happens.

We cannot change things that have happened in our lives, but we can change the way we think about them.

Quick Fix

One of the best things about the past is that it's over. Next time you find yourself looking back at negative things that have happened, STOP and bring your attention back to the present moment.

THE RIGHT TO BE WRONG

Some people feel a strong need to be right and to be heard; they want everyone to see things from their perspective and to agree with them. Not many people want to be told what to do or think. Most of us prefer to come to our own conclusions.

Challenge

Replace the habit of being right, with the skill of listening to other people without judgement or criticism but with an open mind. The way to listen effectively is to be quiet inside your own head, so that you can give your full attention to the other person.

Even if you don't agree, don't waste energy on disagreeing for the sake of it. There's a time and a place for healthy discussion, but life becomes easier when you save your opinions for these times, rather than preaching to deaf ears.

STEPPING OUT OF THE COMFORT ZONE

Like children who are afraid of the dark, we cower under our comfort blankets and tuck them tightly under our chins, praying that the dark won't sense our vulnerability and consume us. We feel safe as we hide our heads, roll our feet up in the covers and quiver with fear, hearts racing. If we stay still for long enough and pretend that nothing's out there, everything will go away, won't it? Then we'll be safe.

Snapshot

As a little girl, Elizabeth loved to cocoon herself inside her duvet, but one night she was so uncomfortable with the stifling heat that she slept with her arms outside the covers. She awoke with a start as she felt a needle-like sting. Her hand throbbed, pain shot up her arm and she ran crying to her mother. She'd been stung by a night-crawling wasp. The abject fear she then felt of sleeping with her arms outside her covers lasted for longer than she would care to mention!

Has this misfortune happened to her twice? No. What are the chances of it happening again? Slim. Is it something she still thinks about? Occasionally.

From a young age, we learn what makes us feel safe and secure and even into adulthood, we keep our protective barriers and crutches, because we think we'd fall down without them.

Daring to do something different is like having your arms outside the covers and leaving yourself vulnerable to a wasp attack. Most people would prefer to guarantee they were stifled under the covers, living mediocre lives, than risk stepping outside their protective comfort zone to seize happiness.

HALF EMPTY OR HALF FULL?

Remember the question about whether a glass

is half full or half empty? People who look at the glass as half empty will often put all their focus on the worst-case scenario, whether it's a rejection letter from a potential employer, a rejection from a member of the opposite sex or being turned down by a bank for a loan application. These people will let these possibilities go over and over in their heads making them seem more real.

But those who see the glass as half full don't focus on the fear but on the opportunity; the chance of new contacts or the possibility of meeting the partner of their dreams.

> **There are two ways to live your life. One is as though nothing is a miracle. The other is as though everything is a miracle.**
>
> Albert Einstein

When we are fearful, freezing up and focusing on the worst that could happen, we won't get anywhere. If we don't face our fears, they will keep coming back to haunt us, until we're brave enough to do something about them. I think we often need to look our fears in the face to see that there's nothing there; to see that irrational fear is just False Evidence Appearing Real. Hiding under the duvet, rationalising that if you can't see it then it can't see you, is not the answer.

Some people are so locked into what they're afraid of that they can't see this for themselves. They will deny that they're afraid of making a mistake or scared of growing old alone, and whilst they ignore it, the roots of their fear sink further inside them. Most of us know what it's like to feel the grip of fear and probably think that it's impossible to uproot it. It's so easy with our irrational fears to Forget Everything And Run.

But how many of us have contemplated how we'd feel if we uprooted those fears and set ourselves free from them?

Quick Fix

Take a fear that is currently affecting you in a negative way and answer the following questions:

What's the worst that could happen if I take a risk and face up to the fear?

....

....

....

....

What's the best that could happen if I take a risk and face up to the fear?

....

....

....

....

Weigh up your options and see which one is more appealing to you.

....

....

....

....

When you are in the midst of feeling frightened about something, if you take the time to stop and ask yourself the two questions above, you will realize that you actually have a choice about what you focus on: the best or worst-case scenario. Once you can face the worst-case scenario and accept it, you can take action to avoid it and get on with making what you want happen. Too many people invite the worst to happen: because they think about it and put their energies into it, they draw it to them like a magnet. Put your focus on what you want to happen and then let it happen.

Quick Fix

Why don't you put the same amount of time and effort that you've been investing in destructive activities, thoughts and fears into making yourself secure?

Remember that you have choices about what you do. You can change the way you act.

THE MILLION-DOLLAR QUESTION

Once you have chosen to become your own security guard and to do things that honour who you are, how do you know what are the right things for you to do?

Tony Adams admits that he missed the odd Arsenal training session to attend an Alcoholics Anonymous meeting. Some may say that he lacked commitment to his team, but what he was doing was putting his sobriety and well-being first. He asked himself the million-dollar question: What's in it for me?

What's in it for you? What can you spend time doing that will make you realize how great you are? What have you always wanted to do?

Bear in mind that no one and nothing has made you feel insecure: you've chosen to feel that way. That doesn't mean you've done it consciously, but for whatever reason you have allowed yourself to feel this way. This puts you in a position of great power because it means that you - and only you - can make yourself feel secure. And if it's only up to you, what are you waiting for? Start now!

No one can make you feel inferior without your permission.

Eleanor Roosevelt

Challenge

What's in It for Me?

Do things that...

- make you smile
- make you laugh
- energize you
- relax you
- focus on your talents
- help you meet like-minded people
- allow you to give to others
- give you something to tell your grandchildren
- you enjoyed doing as a child
- make the most of your potential
- you can enjoy on your own

If you don't know what these things are yet, have some fun experimenting. Adams found enjoyment in many things that were far removed from alcohol: literature, theatre, spending time with his children, learning French, playing the piano and studying for a Sports Science degree. You don't have to be the best at everything – just enjoy the new experiences.

Quick Fix

With everything you do from now on, ask yourself the simple question: 'What's in it for me?'

Chapter 11
How Does Your Garden Grow?

When you give something up, what do you gain? When you gain something, what do you give up? Almost everything in life works on an exchange mechanism of one in, one out: you leave one job to start another; you move house to live somewhere else; you spend money to get something in return; and, as you know, you give up negative habits to make way for healthier and happier ones.

During my many years' work as a personal trainer, I realised that most of my clients wanted to lose weight and I took the knowledge and experience I gained to develop a weight-loss programme called Lighten Up. The idea behind Lighten Up, that makes it different from other programmes, is that weight loss starts in the head and then moves down the body. I always say to people that they've got to shed their negative beliefs to be able to shed the extra pounds. But what has this got to do with Life DIY?

When working with people who want to lose weight, one of the first things I ask them is how they think they're going to do it. Usually the first word they spit out is 'dieting'! So I then ask them how much dieting they've already done and the answer is usually 'Loads!' And then I ask them how many of these diets have worked in the long term and 99 per cent of the time they say, 'None!'

The interesting thing is that most of these people worked out a long time ago that diets aren't the answer to permanent weight loss, yet they continue to jump on the overloaded bandwagon of the latest diet fad, only to fall off, often a few pounds heavier, further down the road. So, even once I've convinced people that following the same old diets is unlikely to work again, they still think that just giving up certain things like chips, chocolate, alcohol, cream cakes, midnight cookie binges, takeaways, greasy fry-ups, will do the trick. Now I'm not saying that cutting out some of these things won't make a difference, but I've seen people restrict their diets and still fail to become slimmer. So what is the answer? What else do they have to give up and what else do they gain?

Picture a garden: trees, grass, flowers, shrubs, weeds, insects, birds and maybe a pond or vegetable patch. Now I don't claim to be an expert on gardening, but I do know that cultivating a beautiful garden requires time and patience and I also know that you have to get rid of the undesirable weeds to make room for beauty. You have to prepare, and preparation takes time and energy.

The time is always right to do what is right.

Martin Luther King jr

Anything we want to grow needs a similar tactic: whether we want to grow a healthy, fit, slim body or a positive, infectious attitude to life, we need to pull out whatever weeds are getting in our way. We need to give up the negative comfort zones and realize that just because we've spent a lot of time investing in them, we don't have to keep doing so. There is another way.

HOW TO WIN THROUGH LOSING

Client case study

Megan came to me for help with her weight. She had been overweight for many years and had reached a point where she was so uncomfortable with her body that she felt compelled to do something about it. Whilst lodged in this terrible discomfort, she was also terribly safe and cocooned by the way she led her life. She'd behaved like an overweight person for most of her life and had an autopilot setting for overeating and being underactive.

Megan knew what she wanted to gain: she wanted to be shapely and fit and to feel attractive again. Other than body fat and a few dress sizes, she hadn't thought about what she would lose - what she'd have to get rid of to achieve her goal. When I asked her to think about this, she looked a little confused - surely a slim physique would just lead to her gaining more from life?

What Megan had not yet understood was that she would literally need to declutter the weight from her mind first before she could permanently let go of it from her body - after all, what was making her hold on to the weight was the emotional hook which led her to overeat and under-exercise. She'd have to lose her emotional attachment to food, her status as a champion couch potato and her versatile 'It's because I'm fat' excuse for not achieving.

With some help from me, Megan saw that she was still blaming her mum for overfeeding her and that she also had a lot of anger towards others to throw out. Once the anger, blame and excuses stopped, there were no more mental parasites to feed and she could finally learn to listen to what her body truly wanted and needed.

Losing weight - or slimming, as I prefer to say - is about listening to your body as you did when you were a baby. We all started life with the innate ability to acknowledge hunger and thirst, satisfy our cravings and then carry on with whatever we were doing. We can regain this, but what we need to do first is weed out the beliefs that we have about food and our bodies.

A belief that the majority of dieters hold on to is that becoming slimmer and healthier is hard. The very fact that they think this, means that it will be so! They colour their future efforts with their past failures rather than saying, 'Hey, that dieting thing really didn't work, but at least I know that now and can stop doing it – yippee! '

You'll only win when you've lost whatever's holding you back.

Challenge

What do you want to gain? What do you think you will have to give up to do it? Write down all the mental comfort zones, habits and beliefs you think you will need to give up in order to gain what you want. Be really honest with yourself! There are some examples below:

GAIN

1. Being more positive.

2. Feeling better about myself.

3. ....

4. ....

5. ....

6. ....

7. ....

8. ....

9. ....

10. ....

GIVE UP

1. Being negative.

2. Putting myself down.

3. ....

4. ....

5. ....

6. ....

7. ....

8. ....

9. ....

10. ....

Are you prepared to give up what you have to?
Are you ready to take on what's necessary?

YOU ARE WHAT YOU THINK YOU ARE

It never ceases to amaze me how much people want to keep hold of things that cause them difficulty or pain. They'd rather carry these burdens about, because they're used to them, than feel something different.

If you think that this applies to you, pay attention to what I'm going to say next: to DIY your life you have to be prepared to swop your mindset. Are you prepared to do that? Yes, you! Will you really work at changing how you think? Will you really drop some of the thoughts that are limiting you?

Client case study

Let's go back to Megan for a moment. She was very proud to tell me that she had lost significant amounts of weight twice on different diets in the past. Whilst I congratulated her on her willpower, I was more interested in what had caused her to regain the weight. She said that she had never truly enjoyed having a slimmer physique because she always expected the weight to return.

What a self-fulfilling prophecy! You believe something will happen and lo and behold, it does! It's no wonder Megan's weight returned to her. Together we had hit upon a very important weed that Megan needed to uproot.

From early on in life we cultivate ideas, turning them into deep-rooted beliefs, and some of them turn out to be weeds. As children we accept what we're told, so we don't recognize the weeds. As adults we can make the distinction. Look back at these ideas and see how ridiculous they are:

- Children should be seen and not heard.
- Big boys don't cry.
- Polo mints make you sterile.

- Watching TV gives you square eyes.
- Eating crusts of bread makes your hair go curly.

Equally ridiculous to me are some of the beliefs that stop people from changing:

- I don't have time/energy.
- I'm not good enough.
- It's going to be difficult.
- I'm not ready.
- I've been like this for too long.
- It's too late to change.
- I don't deserve to be happy.
- Life is hard.
- It's not me who needs to change.

Some of these may seem familiar and I'm sure that you have your own you could add, but what I'm more concerned with now is how we change these thought patterns. That's all these beliefs are – habitual thoughts. And the most effective way to change the way you think is to replace the thoughts and beliefs you no longer want with the ones you do want. In this way, you weed out the old ones and plant new ones at the same time.

WEEDING OUT THE NEGATIVES AND GROWING THE POSITIVES

Some people say that the best thing you can do to ensure happy and healthy plants is to talk to them and even sing to them! A few of you may be panicking now that I'm going to have you hugging trees and dancing around them. Well, stay calm. There's no tree-hugging in this workbook, but there is some talking to be done: I want you to talk to yourself.

As you now know, talking to yourself is not a sign of madness we all do it. I lived in the centre of London for many years and decided not long ago that I wanted to move to somewhere quieter, surrounded by nature. Whilst I had enjoyed my time in London, I had come to appreciate that the most valuable thing that I had was my own space and so I moved out of the city. I remember the first night I spent in my new home. It's in the middle of the countryside and is very peaceful. I got into bed, turned off the light and couldn't believe how loud it was. Where was this din coming from? I just couldn't work it out. It was coming from my head. Living in the hustle and bustle of London I had failed to notice that it was just as noisy in my own head as it was outside.

As you also know now, the key to talking to yourself is what you say. And this is where affirmations come into play. You will have noticed that there have been affirmations throughout this workbook and they have played a part in a few of the challenges. I also asked you right at the beginning to suspend judgement and said that I would come on to talk about why I think affirmations are so important. So, here we go.

FACING THE SUNSHINE

Most plants grow towards the light that feeds them and we grow towards the thoughts that we feed ourselves. So if your thoughts are focused on what you don't want, don't be surprised to find yourself heading towards it. You get what you focus on.

> *Keep your face to the sunshine and you cannot see the shadow. It's what sunflowers do.*
>
> Helen Keller

Children focus their attention on laughter, fun, games, discovery, adventure, love, kisses, cuddles, colourful stories and happy endings. Most adults concentrate on what's wrong, what's missing from their lives, stress, guilt, worry, anxiety and struggles. All you have to do is watch a soap opera to see a mirror image of your thoughts. Notice how you feel after you've watched one. I would guess pretty drained and low. But what happens when a child finishes a storybook? They want to read it all over again!

My experiences with clients have taught me that there's one very important belief to have when working with affirmations and it's this: Affirmotions work! If you don't believe in them from the start, and mutter them through gritted teeth while rolling your eyes, then forget it. I'm not saying that sitting at home and chanting is all you have to do, but I do know that talking to yourself in a positive, encouraging and nurturing way as well as acting differently will make a difference. The catch is that unless you do it, you won't know how important it is. So what have you got to lose?

Quick Fix

I want you to read the following sentences
and write down the first thing you think of.

- Don't think about cheese.
- Don't smile.
- Don't look up.
- Don't imagine a purple balloon.
- Don't picture a naked person.

Well, that should have got you all in an altered
state! What you will have noticed is that you
thought about the very thing I asked you not to
think about.

When you use negative statements like 'Don't
let that wind you up', 'I mustn't have another
drink', 'Stop annoying me' or 'I don't wont to be
fat any more', your brain has first to think of what
you don't want before it can delete it, so it thinks
about being wound up, another drink or rolls of
fat. Your thoughts are like boomerangs what you
send out comes flying back at you. So how can
you make it easier on your brain?

Think of some of the things you often catch
yourself saying inside your head and then think
about how you can change their focus. Avoid any
words that make you think of the negative at all.
For example, if your mantra has been 'life is hard'
then saying 'Life's not that hard' still conjures an
initial image of life being hard, but 'Life is easy' has
a whole different slant. You might find this strange
at first and you may experience some internal

resistance, but the more you say this, the more your brain thinks about how easy things can be rather than having to delete the idea of struggle. Notice how different you feel when a statement has a positive focus.

GROWING A POWERFUL BELIEF

Beliefs are fundamental to success in whatever realm; in fact many people believe that the belief that you can do something, is more important than your actual ability. Look at Megan on her quest for a slimmer body. Because she'd always believed that the weight would return, once she achieved a certain weight loss, she would start to act like a fat person again because that's what her belief directed her to do. And what do you think happened?

The power beliefs have to affect the way we act, is similar to the placebo effect, i.e. something works because we believe it will. Recent research shows that, for certain ailments, placebos work in up to 90 per cent of cases. This is because our thoughts have a direct effect on how we feel and how we feel affects our bodies and actions. Just notice what happens when you think of something that makes you angry or anxious: there's no denying that there is a very real physical effect. Now picture someone you love: you get an instant wave of calm and happiness. What do you think is better for your health?

Research shows that both our thoughts and our self-talk are based on our beliefs, which can exist with or without evidence that they're true

(Grainger, 1989). Beliefs shape the way we talk to ourselves, which in turn affects our self-esteem.

> ***One person with a belief is equal to a force of 99 with only interests.***
>
> John Stuart Mill

So, let's get on with nurturing some beliefs. The next exercise is sure to put a smile on your face!

Challenge

PART ONE

1. Write down in your Sort Your Life Out Journal as many instances as you can of when you:

- did something really well
- were praised for a task
- gave 100 per cent effort to a job
- learned a new skill
- persisted in the face of difficulty

Write down anything, no matter how small or everyday it seems: passing your driving test, dealing with a difficult person, getting a job, telling someone how you felt, buying a house, learning to be on your own, organizing a project, making a card or present for a loved one. Take as long as you want to do this - even keep adding to the list for days. I want you to find about 30 things.

2. Read through your list as though it were someone else's achievements.

3. Choose the five things of which you are most proud, which give you a great feeling and show how diverse your skills are.

4. Imagine you're going to put together a movie sequence. Place these events in an exciting order (not necessarily chronological).

Challenge

PART TWO

You may find it easier to do this part with your eyes closed. Maybe record yourself reading it through and play it back, get someone else to read it to you or go through it several times until you're comfortable doing it without the book.

5. Sit comfortably and think of a time when you felt really in control and relaxed. Take yourself back to that time and relive it until you feel that way again.

6. Imagine you are about to watch a movie in which you're the star, a movie of your greatest achievements. Take your seat in the cinema now.

7. Slowly watch that movie on the big screen in front of you from beginning to end, paying particular attention to the star of the show.

8. You have a control panel in front of you, that allows you to change every quality of the movie. Use your controls now to make that movie as powerful and exciting as it can be for you. Change the sound or volume, maybe add a music soundtrack, alter the colour or contrast, make the screen bigger or smaller, move the screen closer to you or further away. Play around with these variables until it can't get any better!

9. Watch the movie again and notice how each event makes you feel. Look at the leading role and think about how well that person has done!

10. Repeat this at least five times then stop.

11. Take a few deep breaths and slowly bring your attention back to wherever you are.

Challenge

PART THREE

12. Now write a critique of the star performance. What are the qualities of the person you were watching? Think back and answer the following questions. Write your answers in your notebook or on the opposite page.

- What would you say about that person?
- What are their most outstanding qualities?
- Do they persevere?
- Are they focused on what they do?
- Are they full of self-belief?
- What makes that person special?

13. Turn your answers into powerful statements, e.g 'They've got what it takes', 'They can do whatever they want', 'They've got so much drive and energy.'

14. You're about to leave your seat in the cinema and enter the movie yourself, but before you do that, alter the statements you just wrote so that they are about you: 'I've got what it takes', 'I can do whatever I want', 'I've got so much drive and energy.'

15. Step inside the movie now and experience those events all over again, seeing them through your own eyes. See what you saw, hear what you heard and feel what you felt in each instance.

16. When you get to the end, start again and add the positive statements you wrote about yourself, saying these if you really mean them.

17. Repeat this at least five times, making each run-through even more powerful and exhilarating than the last!

> 18. Then take a few deep breaths and bring
>   your attention back to wherever you are,
>   bringing with you those fantastic feelings!

Chances are you've never done anything like this before. It may feel strange at first, but it gets better with practice! Anytime you want a hit of energy, take five minutes to repeat this exercise. Focus on your statements because these will be very personal affirmations that you know will increase your self-belief. You can't go through life relying on hearing these things from other people, you could be waiting a long time! And the cool thing is that you know them to be true!

> **Affirmation**
>
> I am flexible and open to change.

HOW TO FEED YOUR BELIEFS WITH AFFIRMATIONS

If you plant seeds, you feed and water them and are patient with them. You don't shove them in the ground and yell, 'Come on, hurry up and growl' How do you feed and water your beliefs? Here are some top tips:

*   **Repeat:** When you repeat affirmations, you are rooting them in your brain. Say an affirmation at least 100 times a day.

*   **Time:** Plant your affirmations when they will be most useful to you. For example, to keep calm before a presentation, you can say 'I'm

eloquent and calm' for days beforehand, but saying it just before you deliver will add extra power.

- **Action:** Act on your affirmations to prove their truth. If you say 'I choose not to smoke' then honour that by not buying cigarettes, throwing out your lighter and avoiding smoky places. Thinking and doing are much more powerful when they're entwined.

NOURISHMENT

The Life DIY process is about treating yourself with more respect as you learn to appreciate who you are. Effective Life DIY is not just about changing the way you think, but also about changing the way you treat your body. It's important to consider the physical benefits you'll get from being more active and improving the quality of the food you eat.

MOVE IT OR LOSE IT!

Convincer

What is your body designed to do? It's designed to move, that's why you have muscles, joints, ligaments and tendons. Your body wants to be active!

The benefits of being active are endless: not only do you seriously reduce your risk of illness (e.g. diabetes, heart disease, various forms of cancer, obesity) but activity also triggers the brain to secrete feel-good hormones, which is the body's way of making you feel high.

Inactivity is a fast track to the health problems and weight gain that are often key reasons why people don't feel good about themselves.

Quick Fix

Did you know that one of the best ways to change your mental state is to change your physical state?

Next time you are in a situation in which you feel tense, stressed or anxious, get away from it. Do some activity, even if it's just going for a quick walk.

Notice how your mood changes as you move your body.

How many hours a week do you think the average person spends watching television? Twenty-six hours. The environment we live in doesn't encourage us to be active: we don't have to work the land or hunt for our food; in fact you can even have it delivered to your front door.

Many people have just got into the habit of being inactive and of eating the wrong food - and too much of it. Habits are like deep holes: easy to fall into and hard to get out of. But the great thing about them is, that they're only things that you do. You can do something different.

Quick Fix

Think about the feeling you have after you've been active. How many people do you know who feel bad after a brisk walk for example? Not many! When you don't feel particularly motivated to be active, immediately focus on the feeling you'll get when you've finished, rather than the effort it will take to get off your backside! Then, with the good feeling in mind, go for it!

YOU ARE WHAT YOU EAT

I believe it's true to say we are what we eat. A fresh, healthy, balanced diet is an essential part of living a long life full of vitality and energy. Our bodies need a number of nutrients from different food groups in order to function properly, but too many of us eat too much processed and refined food that lacks key nutrients.

We are natural organic beings and the more food we eat that is in or close to its natural state - for example fruit, vegetables, wholegrains, lean proteins, essential fats and water - the better we feel. Natural fresh products are best for us because the human body has had centuries of practice at digesting them and can convert them easily into energy. Foods that are pre-prepared and packaged are more than likely to be chemically enhanced or preserved and our gut has only had a few years to get used to these new substances, so they can confuse our bodies and can be difficult to digest, draining energy away from us.

Dietary advice has changed a lot over the last 30 years and a lot of the information seems to conflict. So look to eat several different types of food, always looking for balance.

WATER

Water is an essential part of our bodily needs, second only to oxygen. It is vital for digestion and elimination and helps to flush out toxins. We lose on average 2 litres every 24 hours and need constant replenishment to feel and look good.

Dehydration from lack of water and/or an excess of caffeinated, sugary and alcoholic drinks can have detrimental effects on your mental, as well as physical state. For example, you can experience a lack of concentration and clarity as well as an increase in tension and irritability.

Quick Fix

Look to drink water little and often throughout the day and notice how alert and energised you feel.

One to Watch

THE SHAWSHANK REDEMPTION

Chapter 12
Mental Feng Shui

Feng shui is a term that has entered the Western vocabulary in recent years. As the obsession with our living spaces has increased, so the idea that the place in which you live or work can greatly affect your mood and success has become widely accepted. There are many stories in the East, and now even in the West, of how businesses have turned around their performance with the help of a feng shui expert. These principles are also becoming popular in the home to increase our chances of personal wealth, health and love.

'Mental feng shui' can help increase your chances of a more fulfilling life by balancing the energy flows inside you. I have already mentioned how energy flows through our bodies and how we can keep our energy levels topped up with nourishing activities and thoughts. Physical energy can seep out of you when you have to cope with draining demands. Likewise, blocks and diversions in your mind can congest the flow of thoughts. And so I like to think of mental feng shui as the process of keeping your thoughts engaged in the present without rerouting to the past, future or the dead-end road of negativity.

> **When one door closes another door opens:**
> **but we so often look so long and so regretfully**
> **upon the closed door that we do not see the**
> **ones that open for us.**
>
> Alexander Graham Bell

Have you ever been talking to someone, only to realize that you don't have a clue what they have been saying for the last few minutes? Or have you ever been reading, only to go back over a section because your mind had totally wandered, even though your eyes continued to scan the lines? What happens at times like these is that our heads are so busy with chatter that we can't help but be drawn to what that voice inside us has to say. It reminds me of when I was a child and my Mum would be on the phone when I really wanted to ask her something. I would pull on her sleeve and talk over her until she finally paid me some attention. We often find it hard to shut out the voice that's competing for our attention, yet the key to being totally focused is to make sure that we have control over that distracting voice.

As a result of the work you will have already done, you will be aware of what goes on inside your head, and your affirmations and new empowering beliefs will be playing a major role in shifting your perspective. But that stillness and focus on every single thing you do may still be eluding you.

Before I go any further, I want you to take five minutes to clear your head and to see what it feels like to experience a state of relaxation and flow.

BREATHE EASY...

Challenge

The way to get the most benefit from this exercise is to get someone to read it out aloud to you or for you to record the instructions onto a tape recorder to play back. Take your time and realize that it may take some practice.

1. Right now I want you to take three slow deep breaths, each one deeper than the one before. Notice that by changing the way you breathe, you can relax more.

2. Now let's go one step further. I want you to place one hand just above your belly button and one just below. I want you to take another three or four slow deep breaths, but this time taking in as much air as you can comfortably manage and then slowly breathing out. You are filling the lower apart of your lungs and getting more oxygen into your body. This will help you to relax.

3. Sit comfortably and focus your attention on your breathe so you are breathing between those two points where your hands are.

4. Focus on the difference between an in breath and an out breath as you allow your breathing to become deeper and slower.

5. Think of something you need more of in your life right now - perhaps peace, calm, love, space or energy. As you breathe in, I want you to say that word in your head to allow it in and to focus your attention. As you breathe out, I want you to think about pushing out all the tension and discomfort that you want to get rid of. (If your mind wanders, just acknowledge this and bring your attention gently back to your breathing.)

6. As you breathe in now, imagine you are breathing in from your nose to your toes, and imagine breathing out your discomfort through the soles of your feet.

7. The feeling you have now is the ideal state for change. You are likely to feel more positive and open to the possibility of it. You may feel calm, expectant, interested, alert, ready to go or excited. Choose a specific word to describe how you feel at this moment and practice letting this word effortlessly drift from your lips as you breathe out. Or maybe choose an affirmation and repeat it.

Whenever you are in a stressful situation, repeat these words and allow your breathing to change.

The more you do this exercise, the more you will feel the way you want to. And the better you feel, the more control you will have. You probably breathe about 25,000 or more times a day, so my challenge to you for today and every day is to breathe that little bit more deeply. Make a habit of breathing in this way as often as you can - how about 100 times today for starters?

Convincer

Five reasons why you should practise breathing deeply:

1. It helps you to relax and to keep your emotions under control.

2. It helps you to digest food more easily because it relaxes the digestive system.

3. It helps to expel toxins from the body.

4. It feeds your body with more oxygen which gives you more energy.

5. It helps increase mental awareness and clarity.

GIVE YOURSELF THE PRESENT

Snapshot

I stood open-mouthed and totally still. The man in front of me moved with incredible grace and awesome control. It was as if water was flowing through every cell in his body and

---

he was sending out ripples of calm and tranquillity. His movements looked easy but I knew that they had taken years of practice. The air around him became still too and the hustle and bustle of the park died away, as all my attention was drawn to this small piece of perfection. His body moved to the rhythm in his head and he was completely in touch with every movement he made, each nuance of his tai chi routine. I don't know how long I watched him, as time seemed to stand still. So powerful was his focus that it drew me in and I fed off his peace.

I wonder how many of you have experienced being in a space like this, a place where the rest of the world drops away and the only thing you're aware of is yourself and what you're engaged in. There are different ways this state can be labelled. Many people are most familiar with 'entering the Zone' in the realm of sport. It is considered by many sportspeople to be the pinnacle of their careers - something to be attained only a handful of times. I have worked with many sporting champions and no matter what their sport, it is this idea that fascinates me.

I once heard a very successful and well-known sports personality being interviewed on television. She said that she thought an athlete was fortunate to be able to enter into that space once or twice in their career. Luckily I've had the chance to work with this woman on a number of occasions and after I had met her a few times, I brought up that interview and her comments. I believe that that space, or Zone, is open to anybody at any time.

You don't have to go looking for it because it's always there and it's whether you choose to enter that space or not that makes the difference.

In order to be in the moment and be totally present, you need to clear your mind of mental chatter, although this dialogue isn't always negative, sadly for many its presence is dispiriting for a lot of the time, drawing attention to emotions such as fear of failure, anger, worry, control and the other mental comfort zones.

Tim Gallwey has written a series of books entitled 'The Inner Game'. He says that the Inner Game in any field is played well 'by all those who have achieved excellence in any field, and poorly by those who fail to achieve their potential'. He talks of the two selves that we all have:

Self 1 is the inner critic who looks to the past and future, who doesn't like to lose control and who is a 'phenomenon of mental self-interference'.

Self 2 is the natural self who, if left to its own devices, performs well; this is because it's the 'present' self, or as Gallwey calls it 'the total human organism, the natural entity'. This is the self who dominated our lives when we were very young and is the self who takes over when we are happily engaged in something.

As a self-confessed golf addict, I'm fascinated most by Gallwey's book on golf. Golf, for me, teaches you how to overcome the nagging voice of anxiety, doubt, fear of failure and lack of self-belief. Rather like many aspects of life, it's a game of a person playing against themselves.

After all, how many sports do you know where the aim of the game is to spend as little time as possible actually playing the ball - mere minutes in hours of play - thus allowing the mind plenty of time to wander and distract you?

> **Negative thoughts lead to negative performance.**
>
> Sally Gunnell

What Gallwey noted from all his observations was that when Self 1 (our inner critic) was engrossed in a concentration exercise, it interfered less with the activity and so performance improved. Think about what you do if you want to get someone out of your way: put baby in his playpen so he's occupied and won't vie for your attention; give Grandma a task to keep her out of the kitchen whilst you prepare dinner; keep your children occupied with a video whilst you have five minutes to yourself. Distraction tactics! So how do you keep your mind entertained so it can't get up to mischief?

The conscious mind, clever though it is, can only cope with a certain number of things at any one time. So if you occupy your mind with a concentration exercise, there's no room left for negative thoughts. The mind is focused, absorbed and in a state of relaxed concentration. In the example of golf, Gallwey will coach players to say certain things at key points in their swing; this means that the player is engrossed in talking while just allowing the swing to happen uninterrupted, thus achieving a state of total presence or flow.

> **As long as I can focus on enjoying what I'm doing, having fun, I know I'll play well.**
>
> Steffi Graf

The reason people become champions is because they can switch off their minds and enjoy what they're doing by getting lost in it. The people who never quite make it in sport, even though they have the talent, are the ones who don't learn how to manage their emotions and negative thoughts. So how can you achieve this presence with anything you do?

Affirmation

I am creating peace in my mind.

HOW DO YOU GET LOST?

Many people think that a state of presence can only be achieved by doing something earth-shattering like breaking a world record or running a marathon, but I can assure you that it's some of the simplest things in life that bring this flow. I want you to think about times when you've been utterly lost in the moment of what you're doing: the walls could be falling down around you and you just wouldn't notice! I've listed some common examples:

- looking at someone you love
- reading a fascinating book
- watching a thrilling movie

- making love
- walking by the sea
- playing with a baby or child
- laughing really hard
- doing tai chi
- running outdoors
- staring at a rainbow
- playing a fantastic golf shot
- being absorbed in your work
- meditating
- listening to a piece of music
- playing a musical instrument
- singing (whether you're gifted or not !)
- savouring a glass of sensational wine
- admiring a piece of art
- watching snow fall
- having a really good kiss
- being engaged in conversation
- dancing

Challenge

1. Write a list in your Life DIY notebook or on the opposite page of the things you do that keep you most present.

2. Write down how you feel when you do these things. Words that spring to mind for me are 'joyful,' relaxed', 'energetic' and 'peaceful' - as if everything in the world is perfect for those few moments.

3. Next, jot down what's missing in these moments - maybe it's anger, worry, lack of self-esteem or anxiety.

4. Finally, think about how often you do these things. How different do you think your life would be if you spent more time in this state of absorption and presence?

DON'T RAIN ON YOUR OWN PARADE

Given that the things that keep you the most present are probably those that you really enjoy doing, how much pleasure and fun do you think you would have if you purposefully thought lousy or pointless things whilst you were doing them? Imagine kissing someone and thinking, 'God, I'm useless!' or being in a spot of breathtaking natural beauty and mulling over why you were such a fool yesterday.

Blissful moments should be cherished and maximised. They will have a knock-on effect. Do you think that when you're absorbed 100 per cent in something you love, that you want to overeat, smoke or waste time being angry, sad or anxious?

The way to keep these monsters at bay is to keep your inner critic busy. Distract your mind with a challenge or mantra or see how many things you can observe about what you're doing or where you are.

Snapshot

One Christmas, Sarah was given an electronic game by her parents - nothing like the fancy kit you can get nowadays, but ahead of other toys at the time. She would get lost in it for hours as she challenged herself to save her little frogs from sudden death at the hand of crocodiles and speeding cars. Soon she had worked her way through all the levels and was getting bored. Her concentration would wander and the game started to lose its appeal. So she decided to give herself a new test: playing the game upside down! That was a whole different ball game and her skills were being tested in a different way. When she tired of that, she played with her eyes closed, seeing if she could remember the set moves from the noise of the game! This kept the fun in something for much longer than would usually be the case and it kept her out of harm's way!

You may be wondering what the silly variations on a child's game have to do with keeping you in a present state. Well, we all have things to do that we get bored with or that we don't enjoy doing. We may think that these balls and chains are never going to be anything other than a burden, but you can turn them into a challenge, if you engage the part of your brain that whinges about how boring they are. Perhaps see how quickly you can get through the ironing or the mail or cycle a different way to work to see what you can notice en route.

> **Everyone is trying to accomplish something big, not realizing that life is made up of little things.**
>
> Frank Clark

Researchers have now confirmed that our happiness level depends more on how frequently we experience a good feeling than on a few episodes of extreme pleasure and 'high fives'. Even seemingly minor things like a fine meal, a good joke or a joyful smile can make us feel happy. Make a commitment to give more time to the activities you love doing and that keep you present. However small they seem. Also commit to seeing how much you can stay in the moment when you have less glamorous tasks to fulfil.

What I want you to realize is that when you're completely in the moment, your focus and concentration are so great that you have no room left in your head for whatever usually bothers you!

YOUR WISH LIST

> **Every man dies. Not every man lives.**
>
> Tim Robbins
> (in The Shawshank Redemption)

Too many people, in my experience, go through life without doing all the things that they really want to do. Some people realize this and do something about it, perhaps making a 'Things to do this year' list or a '30 things to do before you're 30' list. There are even television programmes based on this idea now.

Challenge

Imagine you're 90 years old and you're looking back at your life. What do you wish you'd done less of and what do you wish you'd done more of? Based on what you know about your life so far, write down these two lists below, or in your journal.

Things I wish I'd done less of...

....

....

....

....

Things I wish I'd done more of...

....

....

....

....

....

It's unlikely that many of you are 90, so the good news is that you can do something about this deficit of positive experiences.

To keep you moving in the right direction, write a list of all the things you want to do. It doesn't matter whether the things you choose are small or grandiose. You have the rest of your life to do them and you can add to the list at any time. Write down all the things you want to do now.

Do one of them today, or if that's not feasible, take a step towards organizing at least one of them.

Make a commitment to do it and do it for yourself and only yourself!

THE MEANING OF LIFE

What is the meaning of life? Well, that could be an endless discussion, so let's look at what the meaning of life is for you.

From my experience of working with clients, the meaning of life for most people is the meaning they choose to give it, and a common meaning people choose, is that life is hard. By now, though, as part of your Life DIY, you should be replacing that belief with a better one, one that will enable you to learn, discover, be adventurous and have fun, just as you did when you were a child. I know the reality of life changes as we grow up and most people have to work and take on responsibilities, but I still firmly believe that it's possible to enjoy your life.

> ***People rarely succeed unless they have fun in what they are doing.***
>
> Dale Carnegie

This might sound very simple, but in order to do it effectively, we need to recognize our own insecurities and face ourselves. This is what Life DIY is all about. I hope by now you are feeling that your life is well on the way to complete renovation!

Challenge

This would be a good time to return to the Happiness Equation on page no 79. Work through the equation again, then compare your answers to your first scores to see what progress you've made throughout the Life DIY process.

How did you do? Whatever your score, you will be able to use it to assess where to focus your attention going forward. When you've finished the 12 steps, you still need to continue the Life DIY process. You can go through the book again or use it as a resource.

Affirmation

Life is wonderful.

One to Watch

IT'S A WONDERFUL LIFE

My Story

Everyone has a past and everyone has a story to tell. My past is full of both positive and negative experiences that have made me the person I am today. I want to share my story with you because it probably has some similarities with your own and I want it to give you hope and inspiration that you can overcome your past.

IN THE BEGINNING ...

I was born on 13th May, 1970. I was in such a rush to arrive and get on with life that I was born four weeks premature. I was in a hurry then and I've been in a hurry ever since. Straightaway, I was taken from my mother and put in an incubator because I wasn't breathing properly. Something was wrong with me and as I grew up this would become the strongest belief I had.

I have very vague memories before the age of five, but what I do remember is laughing and wanting to explore and touch things. I was a free spirit - curious and full of fun. My parents found it difficult to deal with me because of my endless energy; they just couldn't keep up, so I was regularly confined to my high chair or, even worse, my playpen. I can actually remember being in that thing and looking through the bars and screaming for someone to let me out. None of the confinement dampened my passion to explore.

Birthdays were fantastic and my parents always put so much effort into making them special. They used to get a clown called Smarty Arty to entertain at my parties. He was a great entertainer: he would make shapes out of balloons and have us running around like dogs chasing our tails. I can remember laughing until I cried and my cheeks went crimson. I was in heaven and these were such great days. I remember asking my Mum, 'Why can't every day be like this?' I don't remember the response.

At the age of five I ran into a few difficulties in kindergarten. Teachers became frustrated with me because my attention span was so short. I hated sitting still and started to fidget and entertain myself by shouting or laughing. This is what teachers call 'misbehaving' and the more they tried to contain and control me, the more I would shout and laugh. I thought that sitting still and receiving instructions was boring and the more they inflicted this regime on me, the more I misbehaved. I really started to get on the teachers' nerves and was often sent out of the room to stand outside. I can even remember being sent down a year to be with the younger children.

This cycle of misbehaving, not concentrating and underperforming was repeated throughout my school life. I was not able to retain information or read or write very well. My Mum had me assessed by an educational psychologist and at the age of five, I was labelled as having severe learning difficulties.

I became frustrated because I wasn't able to do what other kids around me were doing. My frustration grew every time I had to learn anything that involved concentrating. I remember the effort it took me to tie my shoelaces and to learn to tell the time. I hated every second of it and would scream and shout at being forced to learn. My relationship with my Mum started to get difficult. Even then, we were arguing and having shouting matches and our love/hate relationship grew each day as I became convinced that there was something wrong with me.

NOT THE BEST DAYS OF MY LIFE

Through my early schooling things became increasingly difficult and frustrating for me. I was always in trouble for not doing what I was told. According to one of my teachers I was 'disruptive and a nuisance', but it was just because I was bored. I wasn't getting any attention, but I soon got wise as to how to get some: I had to do what I was good at, and that was mucking around and being silly.

My Mum had me reassessed when I was 10 by one of the top educational psychologists in the country. He made me do all these weird tests and answer loads of questions. I vividly remember him talking to Mum after the assessment, as if I wasn't there: 'He has the reading and writing age of a six or seven year old. I advise you to take him out of his school and put him into one with less emphasis on the academic side of things. If he stays where he is, he'll struggle and it's highly unlikely that he'll get any qualifications at 16. Further and higher education are out of the question.'

My Mum, lovely as she is, became more worried and stressed about her son. I was taken out of my school, away from my friends, and put into a state school. I started this school in the second year and didn't really know anyone. I was put in the bottom set for everything, surrounded by others who also had learning difficulties. I hated every second of it and found it even more boring. I continued to pay little attention and that, of course, landed me in more trouble.

I started being bullied by a number of boys who picked on me for being Jewish and having a big nose. This teasing carried on right through my schooling and I felt terrible, hated myself and felt pretty worthless. I remember arguing with my Mum and telling her at every opportunity that I was thick and stupid. Even my best friend started to emotionally bully me and play mind games with me, that fuelled my insecurity.

To make matters worse, I became aware of a physical problem: one of my testicles was getting bigger. I first noticed this when I was about 12 and was too frightened to tell anyone. The testicle got bigger and so did the fear. I hid this from the world for about seven years. I became insecure to the point of paranoia and refused to take off my clothes in front of people. The belief that there was something wrong with me was evidenced and strengthened by what I could see growing on my body.

The turmoil in my head was never-ending. After making and cancelling umpteen appointments with the doctor, I finally plucked up the courage to go. He examined me and immediately explained that he thought it was cancer. I finally had proof that something was really wrong with me. The cyst was removed and, after all that, the biopsy showed that it was benign. But the emotional scar stayed with me for a long time.

At the age of 14, I was so unhappy that I started experimenting with cigarettes and alcohol and then progressed onto drugs. At least when I was 'out of it' I didn't feel so insecure and it was a way of being accepted in a group. This trend would continue right through the rest of my schooling and got to the point when I was on drugs during school hours.

I failed all my exams and left school with no qualifications. I was a dropout.

But something inside me just refused to accept this. I knew that I didn't have to carry on with the mess my life was in and that I could show everyone that I was good enough. And so, I began to turn my life around.

A SECOND CHANCE

I enrolled on a course at a Further Education college. Many of the people on the course were also dropouts with learning difficulties. But I started to apply myself and even began to concentrate. I refused to accept failure and passed the course. My desire to be accepted and to succeed grew. I talked my way into a course that was equivalent to 'A' levels, worked hard over the two years and finished top of the group. I could do better; I could be as good as others; I wasn't as thick as I, and everyone else, had thought.

I carried on my studies and made my way into higher education, learning at establishments that apparently I wasn't worthy of. Armed with three degrees and numerous other qualifications, I have now been on more courses than Tiger Woods. I left university with qualifications in health, fitness, sport science and coaching. I became a fitness trainer and started on my journey of helping others.

BARKING UP THE WRONG TREE

I believed that if I helped other people, then I would be a better person and could prove myself to be good enough. I didn't see that what mattered was that deep down I still felt insecure.

It's strange that working in the field of health and fitness could be so unhealthy for me. I worked myself to the limit: 80 - 90 hour weeks teaching aerobics and seeing lots of personal training clients. The more I came into contact with people from so many different walks of life, the more I realised all the different insecurities and imperfections people have.

I noticed that my own insecurities grew as I started to do more and more personal training. I really didn't feel good about myself and found it hard to deal with the fact that clients were paying me; I wasn't worth it. But regardless, I felt accountable for all of these people and took all of my work very personally, believing that it was not only my responsibility to make these people fitter but also to sort out their lives for them.

I felt so much for my clients, especially the ones who had struggled as much as I had, that I would often dream about them. I would counsel them, listening as they poured out their problems. I made myself available to these people to the point where I really was working 24/7. I believed I had to fix these people.

In addition to all this, I became obsessed with my own appearance and worked out at every opportunity. I pushed and pushed myself. I also continued studying, doing courses in counselling and other areas of personal development including hypnosis and Neuro-Linguistic Programming.

I kept on fighting to seek recognition, wanting people to tell me that I was good enough. Even though I became well known in the health industry, the success of my clients and compliments from others only temporarily inflated my self-esteem. Nothing I did really changed the way I felt about myself.

I developed a 12-week weight-loss programme called Lighten Up. This was a course that helped people not only with the physical and nutritional side of weight loss, but also with the mental aspect. I put my heart and soul into these courses and they started to become very popular as news of their success spread like wild fire. My life was still my work and I didn't realize what I was doing to myself. From the moment I opened my eyes in the morning until I shut them at night, I would be working or thinking about work. I gave and gave and gave, but I never put back.

I was at the beck and call of so many people and my phone never stopped ringing, but I just kept on going. I even managed to write a book that was published by a small publisher in Wales (all the big publishing companies had turned me down). My life got to the stage where something had to give and that something was my health.

THE PROVERBIAL STRAW

One day I was competing in a crazy fitness challenge that I had spent months preparing for. It involved pushing your body to the limit and, on this particular day, my limit was low. I had the 'flu and never should have done it, but again I wanted to prove to the world that I was good enough. My cup was empty and still I was trying to get something out of it.

I collapsed halfway through the challenge and there began the downturn in my health that lasted for nearly 10 years. I developed what doctors call chronic fatigue syndrome and was told to take time off from work, but I didn't because I was self-employed. I carried on running courses, working with clients and doing motivational speaking work. Everyone knew me as someone with boundless energy and I hid my pain well, so most people never even realised. I looked OK on the outside, but felt like death inside. I kept getting rundown and each time this happened, it became harder to deal with and harder to pull myself back up.

In the following years my success increased; more books, work with celebrities, TV appearances and motivational talks. But all of this came at a price. My health deteriorated and the periods of low energy became longer and increasingly more difficult to deal with. The mental clutter in my head became so loud that it frightened me. I had spent years convincing myself that there was something wrong with me and once again I was trying to prove it.

My close relationships with women, my friends and my parents were difficult, as none of us found it easy to deal with my poor levels of energy. I find it hard to admit, but I experienced so many desperate moments that there were times when I almost wanted to go to sleep and not wake up.

For so long, I'd been feeding myself a lie that the more people I tried to help and motivate, the more people would like me and the better I would feel about myself. The truth was, that the more I did this, the more tired I became. There were countless times when I had to perform one and two-day workshops, where I didn't actually know how I was going to get through the days, as I'd only just managed to get out of bed. There was no real quality to my life and inside I was constantly experiencing a cocktail of negative emotions; fear, anger, sadness, anxiety and desperation.

I felt so desperate, in fact, that I continued to look wherever I could for answers as to what was wrong with me and what I could do to get better. I really did try some weird and wacky things, from the conventional to the alternative. I tried a raw food diet, colonic irrigation, strange blood tests, Chinese medicine, Indian Ayurvedic medicine, Bach flower remedies - I even injected my own backside with homoeopathic remedies. I had acupuncture, massages, reflexology and healing. I went on retreats, had liver cleanses and saw a psychic. I practised yoga, toi chi and meditation.

I spent years looking for answers and to be totally honest I don't think any of these treatments made any difference. Occasionally I felt relief when one of the practitioners told me that I had a condition. These diagnoses included various viruses, ME, deficiencies and allergies. But each of these treatments was like sticking a plaster over a deep wound. The plaster would temporarily stop the bleeding and hide the obvious gash, but could never really heal the problem. The problem was staring me in the mirror every day. It was me and my relationship with myself.

FOR PETE'S SAKE

I had spent most of my life giving myself a hard time. I lacked any real faith in myself and honestly didn't feel that I was good enough. I felt like a fraud and a hypocrite, as I was not practising what I preached. I had a low opinion of myself and it was this that needed to change.

It was around this time that I met a very special person who started to help me on my journey. He said it was about 'taking care of Pete for Pete's sake'. I became aware of what I didn't need in my life and the stuff I had been lugging about in my mental rucksack: the guilt, anger, frustration, fear and worry. These had been weighing me down and eating me up inside. It was time to leave the past behind and get on with enjoying my life.

What I needed to do was to fall in love, and not just with anybody; I needed to fall in love with the most important person in the world, myself.

I started to recognize my needs more and take better care of myself, making friends with the part of myself that criticised me and put me down. But I still didn't notice a change.

I didn't notice any improvement because I refused to accept that change could be so simple and straightforward, that all I had to do was take care of myself. I had had my poor health and other problems for so long and had invested a great deal of time and energy in them. Surely the answer couldn't be that simple?

Of course, it's simple in principle, but that didn't make it easy. You see, in order to take better care of myself - to actually love myself – I had to give up all the mental baggage and get rid of all the insecurities and imperfections that had coloured my life. In a strange way, I felt comfortable with all this clutter, as it really felt like a part of me. Could I change? Could I move on? Could life be better? Could I have more energy again? Of course I could.

This didn't happen overnight, and to be honest with you, I'm still learning how to enjoy being myself. Freeing myself from the build-up of uncomfortable emotions has taken great discipline, as it involves replacing the habit of mentally beating myself up, with the habit of loving and approving of myself.

I started to watch my conveyor belt of thoughts and select the more nurturing and pleasant ones over the hard and harsh ones. Ultimately, I took responsibility for the way I treated myself and started to do things for myself, rather than for others. I started to look at what I could do to make myself feel better and get the most from my life. I knew that the only thing that stood in my way was my thoughts and as I've changed them to positive and encouraging ones, my life has started to change too.

I've learned that life isn't the way it's supposed to be, it's just the way it is. What matters is how we deal with it and make the most of what it throws at us. I hope this workbook helps you to make the most of your life and that your life moves forward in a positive and powerful way.

For more Life DIY Tips, Tools and Tecniques:

Check out my web site at: **www.petecohen.com**

Follow me on twitter at **petecohen_** and Facebook, **Pete Cohen**

Check out my blog at:
www.weightlossguru.com/blog

Pete Cohen AKA The Weight Loss Guru

Lose Weight and Feel Great in Just 28 with Pete Cohen

Are you ready to stop dieting and start living?

Pete Cohen - the Weight Loss Guru - will show you how to take back control of your eating, your weight and your energy levels.

Maybe you just want to get back into your favourite jeans. Or you want to get fit enough to keep up with your kids. Perhaps you've struggled with comfort eating for years? Pete can help you, just as he's helped thousands of people across the world to lose weight and to feel great.

Pete will support you as you break your old habits, develop a healthy relationship with your food, and lose weight. This isn't about counting calories, or feeling deprived. It's about re-programming your mind, so you'll think and eat like a naturally slim person. You'll be amazed at how simple it is to lose weight.

There are;

- No complicated formulas
- No punishing exercise regimes
- No rules just tools
- No counting calories

There is;

- 4 easy to follow steps
- Motivation and inspiration
- A online supportive community
- Meals plans and recipes

The Weight Loss Guru Online Programme is easy-to-use and with the support of Pete and our community of members across the world you can and you will succeed.

Take advantage of our special promo and get the two months completely free. You only pay £9.95 and you get three month unlimited access to this inspirational and motivational programme.

Visit the site today and see some of the amazing results people have achieved and how this programme has helped 1000's of people Lose Weight and Feel Great.

Just go to **www.weightlossguru.com**, click Get Started and use the promo **LIFEDIY**